Enrique's
JOURNEY

Enrique's
JOURNEY

The True Story of a Boy
Determined to Reunite with His Mother

Adapted for Young People

SONIA NAZARIO

Delacorte Press

Visit us on the Web! randomhouse.com/teens

Educators and librarians, for a variety of teaching tools,
visit RHTeachersLibrarians.com and enriquesjourney.com/educators.html

Library of Congress Cataloging-in-Publication Data
Nazario, Sonia.
Enrique's journey : the true story of a boy determined to reunite
with his mother / Sonia Nazario.
p. cm.
ISBN 978-0-385-74327-3 (trade hardcover) — ISBN 978-0-375-99104-2 (glb) —
ISBN 978-0-307-98315-2 (ebook)
1. Hondurans—United States— Biography—Juvenile literature. 2. Immigrant children—
United States—Biography—Juvenile literature. 3. Illegal aliens—United States—
Biography—Juvenile literature. I. Title.
E184.H66N3972 2013
973'.04687283—dc23
[B]
2012038328

The text of this book is set in 12-point Adobe Garamond.
Book design by Trish Parcell

Printed in the United States of America

10 9 8 7 6 5 4 3 2 1

First Edition

Random House Children's Books
supports the First Amendment and celebrates the right to read.

To my husband, Bill

CONTENTS

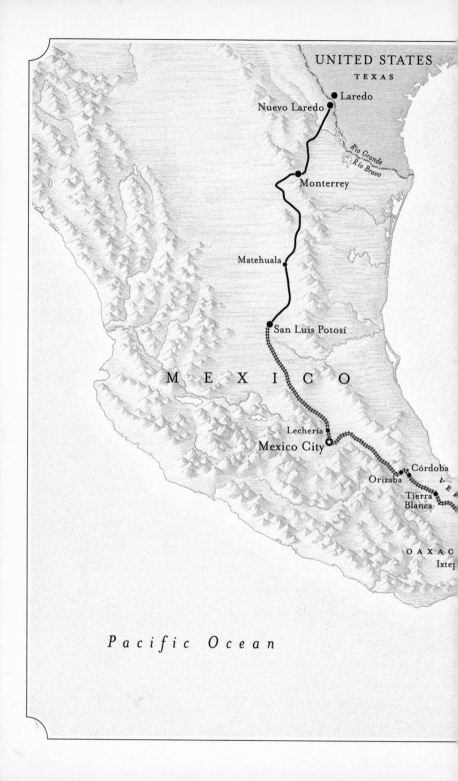

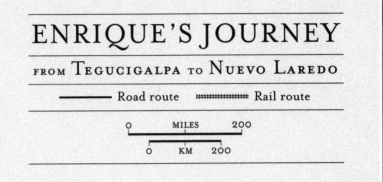

ENRIQUE'S JOURNEY

FROM TEGUCIGALPA TO NUEVO LAREDO

——— Road route   ╫╫╫╫╫╫╫ Rail route

MILES   200
KM   200

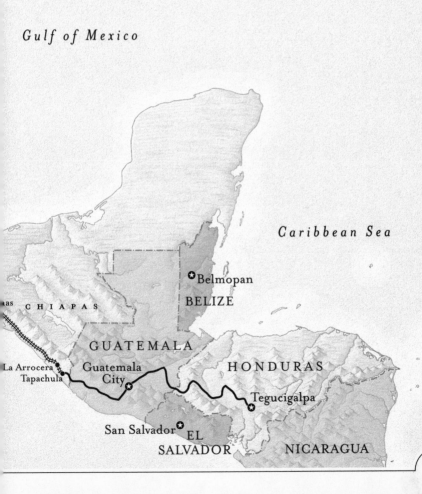

Gulf of Mexico

Caribbean Sea

★ Belmopan
BELIZE

aas   C H I A P A S

GUATEMALA

La Arrocera
Tapachula

Guatemala
City ★

HONDURAS

★ Tegucigalpa

San Salvador ★
**EL
SALVADOR**

NICARAGUA

PROLOGUE

It is Friday morning, eight a.m. A key turns in the front-door lock of my Los Angeles home. María del Carmen Ferrez, who cleans my house every other week, opens the door. She walks into the kitchen.

This early in the morning, I am usually in a frenzy to get out the door and rush to my office at the *Los Angeles Times* newspaper. But on days when Carmen arrives, I shift gears. I loiter in the kitchen with her and we talk.

On this morning in 1997, Carmen and I lean on opposite sides of the kitchen island. There is a question, she says, that she has been itching to ask. "Mrs. Sonia, are you ever going to have a baby?" I'm not sure, I tell her. Carmen has a young son she sometimes brings to watch television while she works. Does *she* want more children? I ask.

Carmen, always laughing and chatty, is suddenly silent. She stares awkwardly down at the kitchen counter. Then, quietly, she tells me about four other children I never knew existed. These children—two sons and two daughters—are far away,

1

Carmen says, in Guatemala. She left them there when she set out for the United States to work. She has been separated from them for twelve years.

Her youngest daughter, Carmen says, was just a year old when she left. She has experienced her oldest boy, Minor, grow up by hearing his voice deepen with age.

As Carmen unfolds the story, she begins to sob.

Twelve years? I react with disbelief. What drove her to travel two thousand miles away from her children, not knowing when or if she would ever see them again? Carmen dries her tears and explains. Her husband left her and the children for another woman. As hard as she worked, she still couldn't earn enough to feed four children on her own. "They would ask me for food, and I didn't have it." Many nights, they went to bed without dinner. She tried to quiet their hunger pangs as she lulled them to sleep. "Sleep facedown so your stomach won't growl so much," Carmen would say, gently coaxing them to turn over.

Carmen, concerned that I might disapprove of her choice, tells me that many immigrant women in Los Angeles from Central America or Mexico are just like her—single mothers who left children behind in their home countries. I start to understand the depths of desperation women face in countries such as hers. In Honduras, for example, most earn $40 to $120 a month working in a factory, cleaning houses, or providing child care. A hut with no bathroom or kitchen rents for nearly $30 a month.

Mothers must send their children to school in threadbare

uniforms, and are often unable to afford pencils or paper or buy a decent lunch. A Tegucigalpa elementary school principal told me that many of his students were so malnourished they didn't have the stamina to stand up to sing the national anthem. Many Honduran mothers pull their children out of school when they are as young as eight. They have them baby-sit younger siblings while they work, or sell tortillas on a street corner.

Carmen left for the United States out of love. She hoped she could make money here and send it back home to provide her children with an escape from the grinding poverty she herself grew up with. She wanted to give them a chance to attend school past the sixth grade. She proudly tells me about the clothes, money, and photos she sends them.

She also acknowledges the brutal trade-offs she has had to make. She feels the distance between herself and her children when they speak on the telephone. As the days go by, she misses important milestones in their lives. Her absence leaves deep wounds. When her oldest daughter gets her first period, she is frightened. She doesn't understand what is happening to her body. Why, the girl asks Carmen, were you not here to explain?

Her children's friends in Guatemala envy the money and presents Carmen sends. "You have it all. Good clothes. Good tennis shoes," they say. Her son Minor answers, "I'd trade it all for my mother. I never had someone to spoil me. To say: Do this, don't do that, have you eaten? You can never get the love of a mother from someone else."

Among Latinos, family is all-important. For women, motherhood is valued far above all else. I was struck by the choice mothers face when they leave their children. How do they make such an impossible decision? What would I do if I were in their shoes? Would I come to the United States, make much more money, and ensure that my children back home could eat and study past the third grade? Or would I stay with my children, even though they would then grow up in miserable poverty?

LEFT BEHIND

A smuggler could sneak Carmen's children over the borders, from Central America into Mexico, and then from Mexico into the United States. But Carmen hasn't been able to save enough to pay a smuggler. Besides, she is afraid to put her children through the dangerous, illegal journey. Carmen was robbed by her smuggler when she trekked north in 1985. She went without food for three days. She knows it could have been worse. Her daughters, she fears, could get raped along the way.

In 1998, the year after Carmen tells me about her family, her son Minor sets off alone to the United States to find his mother. He doesn't tell Carmen he is coming. He hitchhikes through Guatemala and Mexico, begging for food along the way.

He was ten years old when she left. He shows up on her doorstep in Los Angeles thirteen years later. He has missed his mother intensely. He had to know: Did she leave Guatemala because she never truly loved him? How else could he explain why she left?

Minor tells me about his perilous journey hitchhiking. He was robbed and threatened. Still, he says, he was lucky. Each year, thousands of children going to find their mothers in the United States travel in a much more dangerous way. The children make the journey riding on top of Mexico's freight trains. They call it *El Tren de la Muerte*. The Train of Death.

As he speaks, I am amazed by the dangerous journey these children make to try to be with their mothers. What kind of desperation, I wonder, pushes children as young as seven years old to set out, alone, through such a hostile landscape with nothing but their wits?

IMMIGRATION INTO THE UNITED STATES

The United States has experienced the largest wave of immigration in its history. Since 1990, more than 11 million immigrants arrived illegally. Since 2000, a million additional immigrants annually, on average, have arrived legally, or become legal residents.

This wave of immigration differs in one respect, at least, from those of the past.

Before, when a parent came to the United States, usually it was the father. The children were left behind with their mothers. But in recent decades, more divorces and separations in Latin America have left many single mothers with no income from the children's fathers and struggling on what they make to raise and feed their kids. In large numbers, these single mothers decide to leave their children with grandparents, relatives, or neighbors to work in the United States and send home whatever money they can to help their children have a better life.

As Carmen assured me, her experience *is* incredibly common. In Los Angeles, a University of Southern California study showed, 82 percent of live-in nannies and one in four housecleaners are mothers who still have at least one child in their home country.

In much of the United States, legitimate concerns about immigration and anti-immigrant measures have had a severe side effect: immigrants have been dehumanized and demonized. Perhaps, I thought, if I provided an in-depth look at one immigrant—his strengths, his courage, his flaws—his humanity might help shed light on what too often has been a black-and-white discussion.

I thought I understood the immigrant experience. My father, Mahafud, was born in Argentina after his Christian family fled religious persecution in Syria. My mother, Clara, born in Poland, emigrated to Argentina as a young girl to flee poverty and the persecution of Jews. Many of her Polish relatives were gassed during World War II. My family emigrated to the United States in 1960. They wanted to leave Argentina, a country controlled by the military, where expression was limited.

Through my parents' experience, I understood the desire

for opportunity, for freedom. I also understood what it is like to struggle without money. Growing up as the child of Argentine immigrants in 1960s and 1970s Kansas, I often felt like an outsider, straddling two countries, two worlds. On many levels, I relate to the experiences of immigrants and Latinos in this country. Still, my parents arrived in the United States on an airplane, not on top of a freight train. My family was never separated during the process of immigrating to the United States. Until my journey with migrant children, I had no true understanding of what people are willing to do to get here to have that same opportunity and freedom.

JOURNALISM

As a journalist, I love to get inside the action, watch it unfold, take people inside worlds they might never otherwise see. From speaking with Carmen's son Minor, I knew I wanted to smell, taste, hear, and feel what this dangerous trek to the United States is like for children. In order to give a vivid account of the experiences these children went through, I knew I would have to take their journey. I would have to ride through Mexico on top of freight trains.

From Minor, I began to understand just how dangerous this journey was for young migrants. They travel alone—cold, hungry, and helpless, with little or no money. Thousands make their way through Mexico, clinging to the sides and tops of freight trains. They are chased and hunted like animals. Gangsters control the train tops, bandits rule the tracks, and the Mexican police who patrol the train stations rape and rob. Most migrant children are attacked at some point, sometimes several times along the way. Some are killed.

Because they are crossing Mexico unlawfully, they can't climb on top of the trains at the station. They have to jump on and off the cars as they are moving, risking the loss of an arm or a leg. To volunteer myself to go through all this was just shy of nutty.

In short, I was afraid.

Before I took the journey, I needed to learn everything I could about it. What's the exact route migrants take? What are the best and worst things that can happen at each step of the way? The places where migrants face the greatest cruelty? And the greatest kindness? Where are the places along the tracks where the gangs rob, where the bandits kill people? Where do Mexican immigration authorities stop the train?

Might I be the only woman on the train? The scary truth is that female migrants, especially young girls, are likely to be sexually assaulted along the way—even if they have the advantage of traveling with a smuggler. Because of this, mostly men make the journey on the trains.

My original plan was to follow one boy from the beginning of his journey in Central America to the end when he reached his mother in the United States. But I realized this plan wasn't realistic. I can't run as fast as a teenager; I wouldn't be able to keep up, to stick with the boy I was writing about. I'd have to be safe. I would find a teenager who had already made the journey from Central America to northern Mexico and follow him from the border to his mother in the United States. Then I would reconstruct the part of his journey before he made it to the United States, both from his stories and by going back and taking the same journey through Mexico that he had.

I am not a brave person. I avoid danger if possible. I tried to figure out ways to protect myself on the journey, and made one rule: No getting onto or off of moving trains (a rule I broke only once).

A colleague from the *Los Angeles Times* had connections to people in power within the Mexican government. He helped me get a letter from the personal assistant to Mexico's president. The letter asked any Mexican authorities and police I encountered to cooperate with my reporting. Showing a letter from the government helped me get permission to ride atop the trains up the length of Mexico. This letter also helped keep me out of jail three times when I was caught by authorities.

The letter also convinced a migrant rights group in Mexico called Grupo Beta to be a bodyguard of sorts for me. Armed agents of Grupo Beta would accompany me on the trains through the Mexican state of Chiapas, the most dangerous part of the journey. I arranged for the train conductors to know when I was on board. I would tell them to be on the lookout for my signal: I'd wear a red rain jacket strapped around my waist and wave it if I was in dire danger.

FINDING ENRIQUE

The border between Mexico and the United States is guarded by U.S. Border Patrol. These guards aim to catch people sneaking across the border, arrest them, and send them back to the country they came from.

The Border Patrol has calculated that the average child caught coming alone over the U.S.-Mexico border is a fifteen-year-old boy. I wanted to find a boy around the average age who was coming to be with his mother and had traveled on the trains. In May 2000, I scoped out a dozen shelters and churches along the Mexican side of the border that help migrants, including minors. I found Enrique through a nun at a church in Nuevo Laredo, the Parroquia de San José. Enrique had come from Honduras in search of his mother. He was seventeen, a little older than the average unaccompanied child caught entering the United States by immigration authorities, but his story was just as harrowing as those I had heard from other children and teens who had taken the journey.

I needed to find a boy who had a shot at reaching his mother in the United States. In Nuevo Laredo, I spoke with dozens of children other than Enrique, but all of them had been robbed of their mothers' telephone numbers along the way. They hadn't thought to memorize the numbers, and cell phones, not widely used in 2000, weren't available to them. Many of them lived in small towns where telephones of any kind were a luxury. Without a contact phone number for their mothers, their chances of continuing their journey were slim.

Enrique, too, had been robbed of his mother's number, but he remembered one telephone number in Honduras he could call to try to recover it. I decided to stick with Enrique. I spent two weeks with him as he camped by the Rio Grande, the river separating the United States and Mexico. He shared with me every possible detail about his life and his trip north. I noted every place he had gone, every experience, every person he recalled who had helped or harmed him along the way.

I wanted to see and experience the same things he had so I could write about them and let people know what he and children like him go through. I began to retrace his steps, making the journey as he had made it a few weeks before. I began in Honduras, interviewing his family, seeing his hangouts. I took buses through Central America, just as Enrique had done. I took the same path along the rails, traveling up the length of Mexico on top of seven freight trains. I got off where he did, in San Luis Potosí, then hitchhiked on a truck from the same spot in the northern Mexican city of Matehuala, where Enrique had hitched a ride to the U.S. border. To follow Enrique's journey, I traveled more than sixteen hundred miles—half of that on top of seven freight trains.

I found people who had helped Enrique and saw towns and places he had passed through. I showed people a photograph of Enrique to make sure we were talking about the same boy. On the trains were other migrant children going to find their mothers. I interviewed dozens of migrants, as well as experts throughout Honduras and Mexico—medical workers, priests, nuns, police officers. All of this helped corroborate Enrique's story.

I returned to Enrique to compare what we had witnessed on our journeys. I wanted to make sure I was creating a true account. All in all, I spent more than six months traveling in Honduras, Mexico, and the United States. In 2003, to conduct additional research, I retraced the entire journey again, beginning in Tegucigalpa, Honduras. Since then I have continued my research with the family and others.

FOLLOWING A DANGEROUS PATH

During the months I traveled in Enrique's footsteps, I lived with the near-constant danger of being beaten, robbed, or raped. Once, as I rode on top of a fuel car on a rainy night with lightning, a tree branch hit me squarely in the face. It sent me sprawling backward—almost off the train. I later learned a child had been swiped off the car right behind mine, by the same branch that hit me. His friends didn't know whether he survived the vortex of air that drags falling bodies into the churning wheels.

Things weren't much safer by the side of the rails. As I walked along a river in Ixtepec, Oaxaca, I passed through a spot busy with trains and pedestrians under the main bridge crossing the river. It seemed like a safe place to be. The next day, I interviewed a fifteen-year-old girl who had been raped by two gangsters in the same spot I thought was safe.

When I came back to the United States, I had a nightmare

every night: someone was running after me on top of the train, trying to rape me. I had to do six months of psychological therapy to be able to sleep well again.

On the trains, I was filthy, unable to go to the bathroom for long stretches, excruciatingly hot or cold, pelted by rain or hail for hours. Although I often felt exhausted and miserable, I knew I was experiencing only a sliver of what migrant children go through. At the end of a long train ride, I would pull out my credit card, go to a motel, shower, eat, and sleep. These children typically spend several months making their way north. They navigate by word of mouth or the arc of the sun. In between train rides, they sleep in trees or by the tracks, they drink from puddles, they beg for food. The journey gave me a glimmer of how hard this is for them.

With each step north, I became even more awed by the gritty determination these children have to get here. They are willing to endure misery and danger for months on end. All they have is their faith and a deep desire to be at their mothers' sides. They resolve not to return home, to press on no matter the obstacles. No number of police and guards will deter children like Enrique, who go through so much to reach the United States.

ENRIQUE

Enrique's mother left him when he was five years old. Years later, as a teenager, he set out for the United States on his own to search for her.

In 2000, the year Enrique left to find his mother, he was

one of an estimated 48,000 other children and teenagers who left Central America and Mexico to come to the United States, illegally and without either parent. The journey is hard for those coming from Mexico but harder for Central Americans like Enrique: they must make an illegal and dangerous trek not only across the U.S.-Mexico border, but also across the border into Mexico itself. Immigration lawyers say only half of them get help from smugglers; the rest travel alone.

Since Enrique set off, the number of children entering the United States alone and unlawfully from Mexico and Central America has surged to an estimated one hundred thousand per year. The U.S. government has fifty-three shelters in twelve states to detain immigrant children, and in 2012, scrambled to open several new shelters.

Some are as young as seven, though typically the children are in their teens. Many go north seeking work. Others flee abusive families. But most of the Central Americans go north to reunite with a parent. They travel with pictures of themselves in their mothers' arms. Some children say they need to find out whether their mothers still love them. They see finding their mothers as the answer to every problem.

TRAIN-TOP LESSONS

Enrique and the migrants I spent time with gave me a priceless gift. They reminded me of the value of what I have. They taught me that people are willing to die in their quest to obtain what I often take for granted.

The single mothers who come to this country, and the children who follow them, are changing the face of immigration to the United States. They become our neighbors, children in our schools, workers in our homes. As they become a greater part of the fabric of the United States, their troubles and triumphs will be a part of this country's future. My hope is that for Americans overall, this book sheds some light on this part of our society.

For Latina mothers coming to the United States, my hope is that they will understand the full consequences of leaving their children behind and make better-informed decisions. In the end, these separations almost always end badly. Every woman I interviewed in the United States who had left children behind had been sure the separation would be brief. Immigrants who come to the United States are by nature optimists—they leave everything they know and love in hopes of a better life.

The reality, however, is that it takes years and years until the children and mothers are together again. By the time that happens, *if* it happens, the children are usually very angry with their mothers. They feel abandoned. Their mothers are stunned by this judgment. They believe their children should show gratitude, not anger. After all, the mothers sacrificed being with their children, worked like dogs, all to help provide their children with a better life and future.

Reunited, they end up in conflicted homes. In many ways, these separations are devastating Latino families. People are losing what they value most: family and the love of their children.

Children who set out on this journey usually don't make it all the way there. They end up back in Central America, defeated.

"This," a Los Angeles woman who helps immigrants told me, "is the adventure story of the twenty-first century."

Enrique was determined to be with his mother again. Would he make it?

Though his story might read like a novel, it is all true.

Part I

Honduras

1

THE BOY LEFT BEHIND

The boy does not understand.

Lourdes understands, as only a mother can, the terror she is about to inflict. She knows the ache Enrique will feel, and finally, the emptiness.

She says nothing. She can't even look at him. Enrique has no hint of what she is going to do.

What will become of him? He loves her deeply, as only a son can. Already he will not let anyone else feed or bathe him. With Lourdes, he is openly affectionate. "*Dame pico, Mami.* Give me a kiss, Mom," he pleads, pursing his lips. With Lourdes, he is a chatterbox. "*Mira, Mami.* Look, Mommy," he says softly, asking her questions about everything he sees. Without her, he is so shy it is crushing.

Slowly she walks out onto the porch. Enrique clings to her

leg. Beside her, he is tiny. Lourdes loves him so much she cannot bring herself to say a word. She cannot carry his picture. It would melt her will. She cannot bear to hug him. He is five years old.

They live on the outskirts of Tegucigalpa, the capital of Honduras. Lourdes, twenty-four, makes money going door to door, selling tortillas, used clothes, and plantains. Or she finds a spot where she can squat on a dusty sidewalk next to the downtown Pizza Hut and sells gum, crackers, and cigarettes out of a box. The street is Enrique's playground.

A good job is out of the question. Lourdes can barely afford food for Enrique and his sister, Belky, who is seven. She has never been able to buy them a toy or a birthday cake. Her husband is gone. She cannot afford uniforms or pencils. Enrique and Belky are not likely to finish grade school. Their future is bleak.

Lourdes can think of only one place that offers hope. As a seven-year-old child, she glimpsed this place on other people's television screens when she would deliver her mother's homemade tortillas to wealthy homes. On television, she saw New York City's spectacular skyline, Las Vegas's shimmering lights, Disneyland's magic castle. The flickering images were a far cry from Lourdes's childhood home: a two-room shack made of wooden slats, with a flimsy tin roof. The bathroom was a clump of bushes outside.

Lourdes has decided: She will leave. She will go to the United States, and make money and send it home. She will be gone for one year—less, with any luck—and come back to

Honduras, or she will bring her children north to be with her. It is for them she is leaving, she tells herself, but still she feels overpowered by guilt.

Lourdes will have to split up her children. None of her family members can afford to take them both on. Belky will be left with Lourdes's mother and sisters. Enrique will be left with his father, Luis, who has been separated from Lourdes for three years.

Lourdes kneels and kisses Belky, hugging her tightly. But she cannot face Enrique. He will remember only one thing that she says to him: "Don't forget to go to church this afternoon."

It is January 29, 1989. His mother steps off the porch.

She walks away.

"¿Dónde está mi mami?" Enrique cries over and over that night. "Where is my mom?"

His mother never returns to Central America. This decides Enrique's fate.

BEVERLY HILLS

Lourdes has paid a smuggler, or "coyote," as they are called, to help her cross Mexico on buses. She closes her eyes and imagines herself home at dusk, playing with Enrique and Belky under a eucalyptus tree in their front yard. Tears fall. She reminds herself that if she is weak, if she does not make it, her children will keep suffering.

Lourdes's smuggler sneaks her into the United States during one of the largest immigrant waves in the country's history.

She enters at night through a rat-infested sewage tunnel in Tijuana, Mexico, and makes her way to Los Angeles. There, in the downtown Greyhound bus terminal, the smuggler tells Lourdes to wait while he runs a quick errand. He'll be right back. She has paid him to take her all the way to Miami.

Three days pass. The smuggler does not return. Lourdes musses her filthy hair, trying to blend in with the homeless so she won't get singled out by police. She prays to God to put someone before her to show her the way. To whom can she reach out for help? Starved, she starts walking. East of downtown, she spots a small factory. On the loading dock, under a gray tin roof, women sort red and green tomatoes. Lourdes begs for work. As she puts tomatoes into boxes, she hallucinates that she is slicing open a juicy one and sprinkling it with salt.

Soon she finds a job as a nanny. She moves in with a Beverly Hills couple to take care of their three-year-old daughter. Their spacious home has carpet on the floors and mahogany panels on the walls. Her employers are kind. Maybe, Lourdes tells herself—if she stays long enough—they will help her become a legal resident.

Every morning when the couple leaves for work, the little girl cries for her mother. Lourdes feeds her breakfast and thinks of Enrique and Belky. She asks herself: Do my children cry like this? I'm giving this girl food instead of feeding my own children. The girl, so close to Enrique's age, is a constant reminder of him. Lourdes is filled with sadness. Many afternoons, she cannot contain her grief. She gives the girl a toy and dashes into the kitchen. There, out of sight, she lets the tears flow. She cannot take being around other people's children when hers are so far away. She decides she must find another kind of job.

CONFUSION

It is two years since Lourdes has left. Enrique is seven.

Boxes arrive back home in Tegucigalpa. They are filled with clothes, shoes, toy cars, a RoboCop doll, a television. Lourdes doesn't write long letters; she is barely literate and this embarrasses her. She tells Enrique to behave and to study hard. She has hopes for him: graduation from high school, a career, maybe as an engineer. She pictures her son working in a crisp shirt and shiny shoes. She tells him she loves him.

Enrique clings to his daddy, Luis, who dotes on him. A bricklayer, Luis takes Enrique to work and lets him help mix mortar. He shares a bed with Enrique, and brings him apples and clothes. They live with Enrique's grandmother, María Marcos. Every month, Enrique misses his mother less, but he does not forget her. "When is she coming for me?" he asks. "She'll be home soon," his grandmother assures him. "Don't worry. She'll be back."

But his mother does not come. Enrique's shock turns to confusion and finally anger. Her disappearance is incomprehensible.

On Mother's Day, he makes a heart-shaped card at school and presses it into María's hand. "I love you very much, Grandma," he writes.

But she is not his mother.

Enrique looks across the rolling hills to his old neighborhood. Belky still lives there with Lourdes's family. Enrique lives six miles away. He misses his sister. He and Belky hardly ever see each other, but they recognize one another's pain.

For Belky, their mother's disappearance is just as painful. She lives with Aunt Rosa Amalia, Lourdes's sister.

"There are days," Belky tells Aunt Rosa Amalia, "when I wake up and feel so alone." Belky is moody. Sometimes she stops talking to everyone. When Belky's disposition turns dark, her grandmother warns the other children in the house, "¡Pórtense bien porque la marea anda brava! You better behave, because the seas are choppy!"

On Mother's Day, Belky cries quietly, alone in her room. She struggles through the celebrations at school. Then she scolds herself. She should thank her mother for leaving; without the money Lourdes sends for books and uniforms, Belky could not even attend school. She reminds herself of all the other things her mother ships south: Reebok tennis shoes, black sandals, the yellow bear and pink puppy stuffed toys on her bed. She finds comfort in a friend whose mother has also left for the States. She and her friend know a girl whose mother died of a heart attack. At least, they say, our moms are alive.

Aunt Rosa Amalia thinks the separation has caused Belky and Enrique deep emotional problems. To her, it seems that they each struggle with an unavoidable question: How can I be worth anything if my own mother left me?

GRANDMOTHER MARÍA

Enrique's father starts dating a new woman. To her, Enrique is just another mouth to feed, a waste of money. One morning, she spills hot cocoa on Enrique and scalds him. Luis throws her out.

But their separation is brief.

"Mom," Luis tells Grandmother María, "I can't think of anyone but that woman."

Enrique's father bathes, dresses, splashes on cologne, and follows his girlfriend. He plans to moves in with her and leave Enrique with Grandmother María. Enrique tags along as Luis leaves. He begs his father to let him come along. But Luis refuses. He tells Enrique to go back home.

His father begins a new family. Enrique sees him rarely, usually by chance. In time, Enrique's love turns to hate. "He doesn't love us. He loves the children he has with his wife," he tells Belky. "I don't have a dad."

His father notices. "He looks at me as if he wasn't my son, as if he wants to strangle me," he tells Enrique's grandmother. Most of the blame, he decides, belongs to Enrique's mother. "She is the one who promised to come back."

Enrique and Grandmother María share a tiny shack, thirty feet square, in Carrizal, one of Tegucigalpa's poorest neighborhoods. Grandmother María built it herself with wooden slats. Enrique can see daylight through the cracks. The shack has four rooms, three without electricity. There is no running water. Gutters carry rain off the patched tin roof into two barrels. A trickle of cloudy white sewage runs past the front gate. The bathroom is a concrete-lined hole outside. Beside it are buckets for bathing. Two or three times a week, Enrique lugs buckets filled with drinking water, one on each shoulder, from the bottom of the hill up to the house.

Grandmother María cooks plantains, spaghetti, and fresh eggs for dinner. Now and then, she kills a chicken and prepares it for Enrique. In return, when she is sick, Enrique rubs medicine on her back and brings water to her in bed.

Lourdes usually sends Enrique fifty dollars a month. In a good month, she sends up to a hundred, in a bad month, nothing. There is enough for food but not for school supplies and clothes, which are expensive in Honduras. There is never enough for a birthday present. But Grandmother María hugs him and wishes him a cheery *¡Feliz cumpleaños!*

❖ ❖ ❖

Enrique loves to climb his grandmother's *guayaba* tree, but there is no more time for play. At age ten, Enrique is old enough to make money. "Your mom can't send enough," Grandmother María says, "so we both have to work."

On a well-worn rock nearby, Grandmother María washes used clothing she sells door to door.

After school, Enrique sells tamales and plastic bags of fruit juice from a bucket hung in the crook of his elbow. "*¡Tamarindo! ¡Piña!*" he shouts.

At a local service station, he jostles among mango and

avocado vendors to sell cups of diced fruit. He rides buses alone to an outdoor food market. There, he stuffs tiny bags with nutmeg, curry powder, and paprika to sell, then seals them with hot wax. *"¿Va a querer especias?"* he calls out. "Who wants spices?" He has no vendor's license, so he keeps moving, darting between carts piled with papayas in case the police are on the lookout.

Younger children, five and six years old, dot the curbs, thrusting fistfuls of tomatoes and chiles at shoppers. Others offer to carry purchases of fruits and vegetables from stall to stall in rustic wooden wheelbarrows in exchange for tips. *"¿Te ayudo?* May I help you?" they ask shoppers.

In between sales, some of the young market workers sniff glue.

Enrique longs to hear Lourdes's voice. His mother's cousin is the only family member who has a telephone he can use. Because Enrique lives across town, he is not often lucky enough to be at her house when his mother phones. She does not call often. One year, she does not call at all.

Better to send money, Lourdes replies, than burn it up on the phone bills. But there is another reason she hasn't called: Her surroundings in the United States are nothing like the images she saw on television in Honduras. She is ashamed to report how shabby her life is.

Lourdes sleeps on the floor in a bedroom she shares with three other women. Her boyfriend from Honduras, Santos, joins her. Santos works as a bricklayer. Living together is less expensive than paying rent on her own. With him here,

Lourdes figures she can save enough to bring her children within two years. If not, she will take whatever savings she has and return to Honduras to build a little house and corner grocery store.

Then Lourdes unintentionally gets pregnant. She struggles through the difficult pregnancy, working in a refrigerated fish-packing plant, weighing and packing salmon and catfish all day. Her water breaks at five one summer morning. Lourdes's temperature shoots up to 105 degrees. She is delirious.

"Bring my mother! Bring my mother!" she cries from her hospital bed.

She has trouble breathing. A nurse slips an oxygen mask over her face.

Lourdes gives birth to a girl, Diana.

Santos has never shown up at the hospital. He is not answering their house phone. He has gone to a bar to get drunk.

Alone, Lourdes leaves the hospital wearing nothing more than a blue paper robe. She doesn't even have underwear. She sits in her apartment kitchen and sobs, longing for her two children back home, her mother, her sister, anyone familiar. Her homesickness is unbearable.

Lourdes is let go from the fish-packing plant after she is injured on the job. Money is tight.

Santos drinks more and more. He doesn't help with the baby. Lately, when he drinks, he gets jealous and violent.

I will not put up with this, Lourdes tells herself. Their arguing gets worse.

Santos goes back to visit Honduras. He promises that in their home country he will invest the little they have saved.

Instead he spends it all on a long drinking binge with a fifteen-year-old girl on his arm. He never calls Lourdes again. Through friends, she hears that soon after returning to California he and other Latin American workers were caught during a raid by U.S. immigration enforcement agents. He has been deported back to Honduras but is determined to return to the United States. He never arrives. Not even his mother in Honduras knows what has happened to him. Eventually, Lourdes concludes that he has died in Mexico or drowned in the Rio Grande.

On her own, Lourdes cannot make car and apartment payments. Lourdes and Diana, who is now two years old, move into a one-car garage that has been converted into an "apartment." There is no kitchen. Mother and daughter share a mattress on the concrete floor. The roof leaks, the garage floods, and slugs inch up the side of the mattress and into bed. Lourdes can't always buy milk and diapers, or take Diana to the doctor when she gets sick. Sometimes they live on emergency welfare, by which the government pays for medical care and food for people who are destitute.

There are random shootings in their neighborhood. A small park near the garage is a gang hangout. When Lourdes returns home in the middle of the night, gangsters come up to her and ask for money. She hands over three dollars, or sometimes five, so they will leave her alone. What would happen to her children if she died?

Unemployed, unable to send money to her children in Honduras, Lourdes takes the one job available: work as a *fichera* at a Long Beach bar called El Mar Azul Bar #1. As a *fichera,* Lourdes must sit at the bar, chat with male customers, and encourage them to keep buying grossly overpriced drinks for her. Her first day is filled with shame. She imagines that her brothers are sitting at the bar, judging her. What if someone she knows walks into the bar and recognizes her, and word somehow gets back to her mother in Honduras? Lourdes sits in the darkest corner of the bar and begins to cry. What am I doing here? she asks herself. Is this going to be my life?

For nine months, she spends night after night patiently listening to drunken men talk about their problems, how they miss their wives and children left behind in Mexico.

Then a friend helps Lourdes get new work: cleaning offices and houses by day and ringing up gasoline and cigarette sales at a gas station at night. Lourdes drops her daughter Diana off at school at seven a.m, cleans all day, picks her up at five p.m., drops her at a babysitter's, then goes back to work until two a.m. After that she fetches Diana and collapses into bed. She has four hours to sleep.

Some of the people whose houses she cleans are kind. One woman in Redondo Beach always cooks Lourdes lunch and leaves it on the stove for her. Another woman offers, "Anything you want to eat, there is the fridge."

"God bless you," Lourdes says to each of them.

Other bosses seem to take pleasure in her humiliation. One wealthy woman demands that Lourdes scrub her living room and kitchen floors on her knees instead of cleaning them with a mop. The cleaning liquids cause the skin to slough off Lourdes's knees, which sometimes bleed. The work also makes Lourdes's arthritis worse. She walks like an old lady some days.

The woman never even offers Lourdes a glass of water.

There are good months, though, when Lourdes can earn $1,200 cleaning offices and homes. She takes extra jobs, one at a candy factory for $2.25 an hour. Besides the cash for Enrique, every month she sends $50 each to her mother and Belky.

Those are her happiest moments, when she can wire money. Her greatest dread is when there is no work and she can't. Then being in the United States, so far away from home, feels pointless.

To her children, the money Lourdes sends is no substitute for her presence. Belky is furious about the new baby, Diana. Their mother might lose interest in her and Enrique now that she has another child. And caring for Diana will cost money that Lourdes should be saving to reunite with them in Honduras.

For Enrique, each telephone call grows more strained. Their talk is clipped and anxious.

"When are you coming home?" Enrique asks. Lourdes avoids answering his question directly. Instead she promises they will be together again very soon.

Then, for the first time, something occurs to him: If she will not come home, maybe he can go to her. Neither he nor his mother realizes it yet, but this kernel of an idea will take root. From now on, whenever Enrique speaks to her, he ends by saying, "I want to be with you."

"Come home," Lourdes's own mother begs her on the telephone. "It may only be beans, but you always have food here." Lourdes's pride forbids it. How can she justify leaving her children if she returns empty-handed?

She makes plans to become a resident of the United States and bring her children legally. She spends a total of $3,850 on three immigration counselors who promise help. But the counselors never deliver. Some are just con artists who steal her money.

Lourdes scolds herself for not dating an American who asked her out long ago. She could have married him, gotten citizenship, maybe even had her children here by now. . . .

Lourdes seriously considers hiring a smuggler to bring the children but fears the danger. The "coyotes" are often alcoholics or drug addicts. She can't imagine leaving Enrique and Belky in the hands of a stranger. Her own smuggler abandoned her.

Lourdes is continually reminded of the risks. One of her best friends in Los Angeles paid for a smuggler to bring her sister from El Salvador. During her journey, the sister called to give regular updates on her progress through Mexico. Then the calls stopped.

Two months later, Lourdes's friend hears from a man who was among the group headed north. The boat to Mexico was overloaded. It tipped over. All but four drowned. Some bodies were swept out to sea. Others, including that of the missing sister, were buried along the beach. When they unearth her body on a beach in Mexico, she is still wearing her high school graduation ring.

Another friend is panic-stricken when her three-year-old son is caught by Border Patrol agents as a smuggler tries to cross him into the United States. For a week, Lourdes's friend doesn't know what's become of her toddler.

For Lourdes, the disappearance of her ex-boyfriend, Santos, hits closest to home.

"Do I want to have them with me so badly," she asks herself of her children, "that I'm willing to risk their losing their lives?" Besides, she does not want Belky or Enrique to come to California. There are too many gangs, drugs, and crimes.

The danger aside, Lourdes does not have enough money for a smuggler. The cheapest "coyote" charges three thousand dollars per child. A top smuggler will bring a child by plane for ten thousand. She would have to save enough to bring both children at once. If not, the one left in Honduras will think she loves him or her less.

Enrique despairs. He will simply have to do it himself. He will go find her. He will sneak on top of trains, as he has heard so many people migrating to the United States do. "I want to come," he tells her.

"Don't even joke about it," she says. "It is too dangerous. Be patient."

2

REBELLION

Lourdes sells her belongings. In California there is such an abundance of immigrants that employers can pay poorly and treat them badly. Even with two jobs, she can't save.

She wants to start over again in America. She and Diana move to North Carolina. In North Carolina, Lourdes quickly lands a job as a waitress at a Mexican restaurant. She finds a room to rent in a trailer home for just $150 a month—half her rent in California.

Here people are less hostile. She can leave her car, even her house, unlocked. And she meets a man. He is a house painter from Honduras, and they are moving in together. He, too, has two children in Honduras. He is kind and gentle, a quiet man with good manners. He is different from the fathers of her children. He eases her loneliness. He takes Lourdes and Diana to the park on Sundays. For a while, when Lourdes works two restaurant jobs, he picks her up when her second shift ends, so they can share a few moments together. They call each other "honey." They fall in love.

Money from Lourdes helps Enrique, and he realizes it. Her gifts arrive steadily. She sends Enrique an orange polo shirt, a pair of blue pants, a radio cassette player. If she were here in Honduras with him, he knows where he would probably be: scavenging in the trash dump, on a hilltop across town. Lourdes knows it, too; as a girl, she herself had rooted around the dump, where scavengers, some as young as six or seven, stand in a stinking stew of oozing trash, a black cloud of buzzards circling above. She and the other scavengers would desperately sort through piles of filth just to find a piece of stale, moldy bread or some bits of plastic and tin that they could sell.

Enrique sees other children who must work hard jobs. A block from where Lourdes grew up, children gather barefoot atop a mound of sawdust left by a lumber mill. Their faces smeared with dirt, the children quickly scoop sawdust into rusty tin cans and dump it into big white plastic bags. They lug the bags half a mile up a hill. There they sell the sawdust to families, who use it to kindle fires, or to dry the wet mud around their houses. An eleven-year-old boy has been hauling sawdust for three years, three trips up the hill each day. The earnings buy clothes, shoes, and paper for school.

Lourdes is proud that her money pays Belky's tuition at a private high school and eventually a college, to study accounting. In a country where nearly half live on a dollar or less a day, kids from poor neighborhoods almost never go to college.

In one neighborhood near where Enrique's mother grew up, fifty-two children arrive at kindergarten each morning. Forty-four arrive barefoot. An aide reaches into a basket and places a pair of shoes into each one's hands. At four p.m., before they leave, the children must return the shoes to the basket. If they take the shoes home, their mothers will sell them for food.

At dinnertime the mothers count out three tortillas for each child. If there are no tortillas, they try to fill their children's bellies with a glass of water with a teaspoon of sugar mixed in.

Enrique knows that without money from the United States, he could be one of these children. Still, he feels he would rather be with his mother than get the money and the gifts she sends.

Lourdes wants to give her son and daughter some hope. "I'll be back next Christmas," she tells Enrique.

In his dreams of his mother coming home in December, she stands at the door with a box of Nike shoes for him. "Stay," he pleads. "Live with me." He promises when he grows a little older to help her work and make money.

Christmas arrives, and Enrique waits by the door. She does not come. Every year, she promises. Every year, he is disappointed, and his anger grows. "I need her. I miss her," he tells his sister. "I want to be with my mother. I see so many children with mothers. I want that."

When Lourdes tells him yet again that she will come home, he replies sarcastically. "*Va, pues.* Sure. Sure." Enrique senses a truth: Very few mothers return. He tells her that he doesn't think she is ever coming back. To himself, he says: It's all one big lie.

His anger boils over. He refuses to make his Mother's Day card at school. He hits other kids and lifts girls' skirts. When a teacher tries to make him behave by smacking him with a large ruler, Enrique grabs the end of the ruler and refuses to let go, making the teacher cry.

He stands on top of the teacher's desk and bellows, "Who is Enrique?"

"You!" the class replies.

Three times, he is suspended. Twice, he repeats a grade. But he keeps his promise to study. Unlike half the children from his neighborhood, Enrique completes elementary school. There is a small graduation ceremony. A teacher hugs him and mutters, "Thank God, Enrique's out of here." He stands proud in a blue gown and mortarboard. But nobody from his mother's family comes to the graduation.

Enrique is small, just shy of five feet, even when he straightens up from a slight stoop. He has a big smile and perfect teeth.

He makes up for the vulnerability he feels inside, fueled in part by not having a parent to protect him, by putting on a tough image. He starts spending more time on the streets of Carrizal, which is quickly becoming one of Tegucigalpa's roughest neighborhoods. His grandmother tells him to come home early, but he plays soccer until midnight.

Now he is fourteen, a teenager. He refuses to sell spices

anymore. It is embarrassing when girls see him peddle fruit cups or when someone calls him "the tamale man."

When he walks to church alongside Grandmother María, he hides his Bible under his shirt so no one will know where they are headed. Soon he stops going to church at all.

Sometimes Grandmother María pulls out a belt when Enrique is in bed at night and unable to quickly escape her punishment. She delivers one lash for each time he has misbehaved.

"Don't hang out with bad boys," she scolds.

"You can't pick my friends!" Enrique retorts. "You're not even my mother." He keeps staying out late into the night.

His grandmother waits up for him, crying. "Why are you doing this to me?" she asks. "Don't you love me? I am going to send you away."

"Send me! No one loves me."

But she says she does love him. She only wants him to work and to be honorable, so that he can hold his head up high.

But the rest of Grandmother María's family says Enrique has to go: she is an old woman of seventy, and he is too much trouble for someone her age to raise. She knows they are right. Sadly, she writes to Lourdes: You must find him another home.

To Enrique, it is another rejection. First his mother, then his father, and now his grandmother María.

Lourdes arranges for her eldest brother, Marco Antonio Zablah, to take him in. Marco once took in Lourdes when their own mother was struggling to feed her and her siblings.

Enrique still misses Lourdes enormously, but Uncle Marco

and his girlfriend treat him well. Marco makes a good living as a money changer on the Honduran border. He is hired to exchange money from one currency to another. Marco's family, including a son, lives comfortably in a five-bedroom house in a middle-class neighborhood of Tegucigalpa. Uncle Marco gives Enrique a daily allowance, buys him clothes, and sends him to a private military school in the evenings.

His uncle pays as much attention to Enrique as he does to his own son. Together, they play billiards and watch movies. Like his mother before him, Enrique sees New York City's spectacular skyline, Las Vegas's shimmering lights, Disneyland's magic castle on the TV screen.

Uncle Marco trusts Enrique, even to do errands for him at the bank. He tells Enrique, "I want you to work with me forever." Enrique senses that Uncle Marco loves him, and he values his uncle's advice.

But handling paper money is dangerous in a place where money is scarce. One day Uncle Marco's security guard is murdered after a job trading Honduran lempiras. After the guard's death, Marco swears that he will never exchange money again. A few months later, though, he gets a call. For a large commission, would he exchange fifty thousand dollars in lempiras on the border with El Salvador? Uncle Marco cannot resist. He promises that this job will be the last.

Enrique wants to go with him, but Uncle Marco insists he is too young. Marco takes Victor, one of his own brothers, instead. Robbers spray their car with bullets. The car with Enrique's uncles careens off the road. The thieves shoot Uncle

Marco three times in the chest and once in the leg. They shoot Victor in the face.

In nine years, Lourdes has saved seven hundred dollars toward bringing her children to the United States. Instead, she uses it to help pay for her brothers' funeral. Marco had visited her once, shortly after she arrived in California. She had not seen Victor since leaving Honduras.

Lourdes goes into a tailspin. She angrily swears off Honduras. How could she ever live in such a lawless place? People there are killed like dogs. The only way she'll go back now, she tells herself, is by force, if she is deported.

Soon after her brothers' deaths, the restaurant where Lourdes works is raided by immigration agents. Every worker there is caught up in the sweep. Lourdes is the only one spared. It is her day off.

ADRIFT AGAIN

Back in Honduras, within days of the two brothers' deaths, Uncle Marco's girlfriend sells Enrique's television, stereo, and Nintendo game—all gifts from Marco. Without telling him why, she says, "I don't want you here anymore." She puts his bed out on the street.

Enrique, now fifteen, gathers his clothing and goes to his maternal grandmother, Águeda Amalia Valladares. "Can I stay here?" he asks.

This had been his first home, the small stucco house where he, Belky, and Lourdes lived until Lourdes stepped off the front porch. His second home was the wooden shack where he and his father lived with his father's mother, until his father found a new wife and left. His third home was the comfortable house where he lived with Uncle Marco.

Now he is back where he began. Seven people live here already: besides Grandmother Águeda, there are two aunts and four young cousins. They are poor. Nonetheless, Grandmother Águeda takes Enrique in.

The whole family is devastated by the murders of Uncle Marco and Uncle Victor. Enrique grows quiet, introverted. He does not return to school. He shares a bedroom with his aunt Mirian. One day she awakens at two a.m. Enrique is sobbing quietly in his bed, cradling a picture of Uncle Marco in his arms. His uncle loved him. Without that love, he is lost.

THE GIRL NEXT DOOR

At Uncle Marco and Uncle Victor's funeral, Enrique notices a shy girl with cascading curls of brown hair. She lives next door with her aunt. She has an inviting smile, a warm manner. At first, the girl, María Isabel, can't stand Enrique. She is seventeen, two years older than he is. He seems arrogant to her. Enrique persists. Hoping to start a conversation, he whistles softly as she walks by. She ignores him. The more she rejects him, the more he wants her. He loves her girlish giggle, how she cries easily. He hates it when she flirts with other boys. He saves up money and buys her roses, lotions, a teddy bear, chocolates. He walks her home after school from night classes two blocks away. Slowly, María Isabel warms to him.

The third time Enrique asks if she will be his girlfriend, she finally says yes.

They understand each other, they connect. She, too, has shuffled from home to home throughout her childhood, and has been separated from her parents.

María Isabel grew up with her mother, Eva, in a borrowed hut on a Tegucigalpa mountainside. Like Enrique's mother, Eva had left an unfaithful husband. She struggled to keep the family fed.

Nine people slept in the hut. To fit, they slept head to foot.

Neighbors loved María Isabel, the sweet, loving girl who always smiled. She offered to help them with chores and cleaning. By the time she was ten, they could already see she was a hard worker and a fighter.

María Isabel says, "*Mira, yo por pereza no me muero del hambre.* Look, I will never die from hunger or out of laziness."

María Isabel graduated from the sixth grade. Her mother proudly hung the girl's elementary school graduation diploma on the wall of the hut. She knew her daughter was a good student, but she could not afford to send her to junior high. Eva herself never went to school; she began selling bread from a basket perched on her head when she was twelve.

At sixteen, María Isabel moved across town with her aunt Gloria, who lived next door to Enrique's grandmother Águeda. Gloria's house is modest. But to María Isabel, Aunt

Gloria's two-bedroom home is wonderful. Besides, Gloria is more easygoing about letting María Isabel go out at night to an occasional dance or party, or to the annual county fair. Eva wouldn't hear of such a thing, fearful the neighbors would gossip about her daughter's morals.

A cousin promises to take María Isabel to a talk about birth control. Now that she is dating Enrique, María Isabel wants to prevent a pregnancy. Enrique desperately wants to get María Isabel pregnant. If they have a child together, he thinks, surely María Isabel won't abandon him.

EL INFIERNITO

Grandmother Águeda quickly sours on Enrique. She is furious when he comes home late, waking up the household.

Enrique has started hanging out in a neighborhood known as El Infiernito, Little Hell. Some homes there are teepees, stitched together from rags. It is controlled by the street gang Mara Salvatrucha, or MS. The Mara Salvatrucha gang members hold sway over the streets throughout much of Central America and Mexico. Here in El Infiernito, they carry *chimbas,* guns made from plumbing pipes, and they drink *charamila,* diluted rubbing alcohol. They rob bus passengers and assault churchgoers after Mass.

Enrique and his friend José del Carmen Bustamante, sixteen, venture into El Infiernito. They quickly buy marijuana, making sure to leave El Infiernito, which is dangerous. They sit outside a billiard hall listening to music drift through the open doors. Lately the boys have been inhaling glue late into the night, getting high off of the fumes.

They talk about what it would be like to ride on top of trains to *el Norte*. In Enrique's marijuana haze, train riding sounds like an adventure. He doesn't even care if there are *migra* agents shooting overhead, and bandits waiting to rob him. He and José resolve to try it soon.

Enrique tries to hide his drug habit from his family and María Isabel.

One day, María Isabel turns a street corner and bumps into him. She is overwhelmed. He smells like an open can of paint.

"What's that?" she asks, reeling away from the fumes. "Are you on drugs?"

"No!" Enrique says.

One night, Aunt Mirian wakes up to the sound of rustling plastic and a strong chemical smell. Through the dimness, she sees Enrique in his bed, puffing on a bag. He is sniffing glue.

This is the last straw. The family kicks him out of the house to live in the little stone cooking shack just behind the house. His grandmother Águeda used to prepare food here, over an open fire. The walls and ceiling are still charred black. The single window has steel bars like a prison cell and there is no electricity.

Now, living alone, Enrique can do whatever he wants. If he is out all night, no one cares. But to him, getting kicked out of the house feels like another rejection.

María Isabel sees him change. Drugs make his mouth

sticky. He is always jumpy and nervous. His eyes grow red. Sometimes they are glassy, half closed. Other times he looks drunk. When he is high, he is quiet, sleepy, and distant. When he comes crashing down from his high, he becomes hysterical and short-tempered. Sometimes Enrique hallucinates that someone is chasing him. For two especially bad weeks, he doesn't recognize family members. His hands tremble. He coughs black phlegm.

His grandmother points to a neighbor with pale, scaly skin who has sniffed glue for a decade. The man can no longer stand up. "Look! That's how you're going to end up," Grandmother Águeda tells Enrique.

Drogo, one of his aunts calls him. Drug addict.

A TEST RUN

When Enrique turns sixteen, he and José try train hopping for the first time.

To get to the United States, Enrique will have to travel north through Honduras, then Guatemala, and finally Mexico. Enrique and José slip past guards into Tapachula, Mexico's southernmost train depot. Just before they reach the train tracks, police stop them. Enrique prays he and José will not be deported back to Guatemala. Then they would have to sneak back over the Mexican border. The officers rob them but fortunately do not arrest them.

Enrique and José find another train. They clamber aboard as it crawls out of the Tapachula station. José is terrified. Enrique is feeling brave; he jumps from car to car on the slow-moving train. He slips and falls—away from the tracks, luckily—and lands on his backpack, which is padded with a shirt and an extra pair of pants.

He scrambles aboard again. But their journey comes to a humiliating halt. Near Tierra Blanca, a town in the South Central Mexican state of Veracruz, authorities snatch them from the top of a freight car. This time the officers don't care about bribes. They take the boys to a cell filled with Mara Salvatrucha gangsters, then deport them. Enrique is bruised and limping from his fall, and he misses María Isabel.

He and José ride back to Central America in what migrants call *El Bus de Lágrimas,* the Bus of Tears. The bus unloads migrants back across the Río Suchiate in the rugged town of El Carmen. The river marks the border between Guatemala and Mexico, just as the Rio Grande defines the border between Mexico and the United States up north. These buses make as many as eight runs a day, deporting more than a hundred thousand unhappy passengers every year.

A DECISION

It is January 2000. Enrique has sunk deeper into drugs. Enrique promises María Isabel he will quit. He is sick of feeling out of control. He owes money to drug dealers and lives in constant fear of their death threats. He is caught stealing Aunt Rosa Amalia's jewelry. He was going to sell it to pay his dealer back.

Aunt Rosa Amalia is furious. Her husband, Enrique's uncle Carlos, recognizes that the boy is troubled. He doesn't want Enrique in jail, he just wants him to shape up. Uncle Carlos finds Enrique a job at a tire store. He tells the family they must show Enrique love. They must be patient with him.

Quitting drugs is harder than Enrique expected, though. He slips back into old habits. He tries to cut back on drugs, but then he gives in to them. Every night, he comes home later. María Isabel begs him not to go up the hill where he sniffs glue, but he does anyway. He looks at himself in disgust. He is dressing like a slob—his life is unraveling.

Even Enrique's sister and grandmother have urged María Isabel to leave Enrique, to find someone better. "What do you see in him?" they ask her. "Don't you see he uses drugs?"

María Isabel tries to give him support. When they walk by his drug haunts, she holds his hand tighter, hoping it will help. "Why don't you leave your vices?" she asks. "It's hard," he answers quietly.

She loses herself in Enrique. She can't leave him, despite his deep flaws. He is macho and stubborn. When they fight, he gives her the silent treatment. He leaves it up to her to break the ice. More often than not, she gives in. He is her third boyfriend but her first love. Enrique also provides a refuge from her own problems. Her aunt Gloria's son is an alcoholic. He throws things. He steals things. Enrique is her escape from fights at home.

Enrique's shame eats at him. He feels guilt for what he has done to his family and what he is doing to María Isabel. He is clear-headed enough to tell Belky that he knows what he has to do. He has to go find his mother. She is his salvation.

María Isabel pleads with him to stay. She might be pregnant. She tells Enrique she will move into the stone hut with him. She won't abandon him. But Enrique fears if he stays in Honduras right now, he will end up on the streets or dead. His own family is sick of him. They think he is sullying the only thing the family owns: its good name.

His aunt Ana Lucía, Lourdes's sister, speaks bitter words.

"Where are you coming from, you old bum?" Aunt Ana Lucía asks as Enrique walks in the door. "Coming home for food, huh?"

"Be quiet!" he says. "I'm not asking anything of you."

"You're a lazy bum! A drug addict! No one wants you here," Aunt Ana Lucía yells. All the neighbors can hear. "This isn't your house. Go to your mother!"

Enrique pleads in a low voice with his aunt to be quiet. Finally he snaps. He kicks Aunt Ana Lucía twice, squarely in the buttocks. She shrieks.

His grandmother Águeda runs out of the house. She grabs a stick and threatens to club him if he touches Ana Lucía again.

"No one cares about me!" he screams, running away.

Now even his grandmother wishes he would go to the United States. He is hurting the family—and himself. She says, "He'll be better off there."

SAYING GOOD-BYE

Enrique decides he will make the journey to the United States by himself. There is no way he can scrape together five thousand dollars for a smuggler. He sells the few things he owns, his bed and the leather jacket Uncle Marco gave him, so he will have money for food along the way.

He crosses town to say good-bye to Grandmother María. Trudging up the hill to her house, he runs into his father.

"I'm leaving," Enrique says. "I'm going to make it to the United States." He asks Luis for some money.

Luis gives him enough change for a soda and wishes him luck. Enrique wasn't really expecting much more from his father.

"Grandma, I'm leaving," Enrique says when he arrives at his grandmother María's shack. "I'm going to find my mom."

Grandmother María pleads with him not to go, but he has made up his mind. She gives him a hundred lempiras, about seven dollars—all the money she has—and kisses his forehead.

"I'm leaving already, Sis," Enrique tells Belky the next morning.

Belky feels her stomach tighten. They have lived apart most of their lives, but he is the only one who understands her loneliness. Quietly, she fixes him a special meal: tortillas, a pork cutlet, rice, fried beans with a sprinkling of cheese. "Don't leave," she says, tears welling up in her eyes.

"I have to."

Every time Enrique has talked to his mother, she has warned

him not to come—it's too dangerous. But if somehow he gets to the U.S. border, he will call her. "If I call her from there," he says to his friend José, "how can she not accept me?"

He makes himself one promise: Only after a year of trying to get to his mother in the United States will he give up and go back.

Enrique, a kid with a boyish grin, fond of kites, spaghetti, soccer, and break dancing, who likes to play in the mud and watch Mickey Mouse cartoons with his four-year-old cousin, quietly packs up his belongings: corduroy pants, a T-shirt, a cap, gloves, a toothbrush, and toothpaste.

For a long moment he looks at a picture of his mother, but he does not take it. He might lose it. He writes her telephone number on a scrap of paper. Just in case, he also scrawls it in ink on the inside waistband of his pants. He has fifty-seven dollars in his pocket.

On March 2, 2000, he goes to Grandmother Águeda's house. He stands on the same porch that his mother disappeared from eleven years before. He hugs María Isabel and Aunt Rosa Amalia. Then he steps off.

PART II

THE JOURNEY

3

SEEKING MERCY

It is almost sundown in Las Anonas, a tiny railside village in the state of Oaxaca, Mexico. A local field hand, Sirenio Gómez Fuentes, is relieved to be done for the day. As he walks home along the tracks, he sees a startling sight. Before him is a battered and bleeding boy, naked except for his underwear.

The boy is limping forward on bare feet, stumbling first one way, then another.

His right shin is gashed. His upper lip is split. The left side of his face is swollen. His eyes are red, filled with blood. He is crying. He dabs at open wounds on his face with a filthy sweater he has found on the tracks.

It is Enrique. He is seventeen. It is March 24, 2000.

Gómez hears him whisper, "Give me water. Please."

The knot of uneasiness in Gómez melts into pity. He runs

into his thatched hut to fetch a cup of water and a pair of pants for the boy. Then, with kindness, Gómez directs Enrique to Carlos Carrasco, the mayor of Las Anonas.

Enrique hobbles down a dirt road into the heart of the village. He encounters a man wearing a white straw hat and mounted on a horse.

"Can you help me find the mayor?" Enrique asks feebly.

"That's me," the man says. He brings his horse to a stop and stares. "Did you fall from the train?"

Again Enrique begins to cry. When Mayor Carrasco sees Enrique's agony, he quickly dismounts. No matter what has happened, he will try to help, the mayor says. He takes Enrique's arm and guides him to his house, next to the church.

"Mom!" Mayor Carrasco shouts. "There's a poor kid out here! He's all beaten up." The mayor's mother hears his urgent tone and rushes outside. He drags a wooden bench out of the church, pulls it into the shade of a tamarind tree, and helps Enrique onto it.

Enrique's cheeks and lips are swelling badly. He's going to die, Mayor Carrasco thinks.

The mayor's mother cleans Enrique's wounds with steaming water, salt, and herbs. She brings Enrique a bowl of hot broth, filled with bits of meat and potatoes. He spoons it into his mouth, careful not to touch his broken teeth. He cannot chew.

Villagers come to see. They stand in a circle around him. "Is he alive?" asks a stout woman with long black hair. "Why don't you go home?" someone else asks. "Wouldn't that be better?"

"I'm going to find my mom," Enrique says quietly.

Eleven years before, he tells the villagers, his mother left home in Tegucigalpa, Honduras, to find work in the United States. Now he is riding freight trains up through Mexico to find her.

Some of the women in the crowd look at Enrique and think about their own children.

They earn little money working in the fields, usually around thirty pesos, or three dollars, a day. Many of them dig into their pockets and press five or ten pesos into Enrique's hand.

Mayor Carrasco gives Enrique a shirt and shoes. He has cared for injured migrants before. Some have died. Giving Enrique clothing will be pointless, Mayor Carrasco thinks, if he can't find someone with a car to drive the boy to a doctor. If the boy doesn't get medical help, the mayor thinks, he will die.

Over time, the people of Las Anonas have seen many injured migrants like Enrique. They debate whether they should repeatedly pay medical costs to help save them.

Mayor Adan Díaz Ruiz, the mayor of San Pedro Tapanatepec, a neighboring town, is passing through. He tells Mayor Carrasco that he does not think it is worth the time and money for doctors to save travelers like Enrique. "This is what they get for doing this journey," he says of migrants.

Mayor Carrasco disagrees. It is worth the effort and money

to let this boy live. He begs a favor of Mayor Díaz: Lend your pickup truck so we can take this kid to the doctor.

Mayor Díaz finally agrees, calculating that it will cost the government three times more to bury the soft-spoken boy who is on the bench.

Enrique collapses into the seat of the pickup. He sobs with relief and tells Mayor Díaz's driver, "I thought I was going to die."

His head against the window, Enrique sobs, but this time with relief.

PERSEVERANCE

In the past few weeks, Enrique has slept on the ground; in a sewage ditch, curled up with other migrants; on top of gravestones. Once, riding on top of a moving train, he grew so hungry that he jumped forward to the first car, leaped off onto the ground, and raced to pick a pineapple. He was able to reboard one of the train's last cars. Another time, he had gone two days without water. His throat felt as if it was swelling shut. There were no houses in sight. He found a small water trough for cattle. It was frothy with cow spit. Under the froth was green algae. Beneath the algae was stagnant yellow water. He brought handfuls to his parched lips. He was so thirsty that it tasted wonderful.

The thousands of migrants who ride atop freight trains must hop as many as thirty trains to get through Mexico. Many are caught by the Mexican police or by *la migra*, the Mexican immigration authorities, who take them south to Guatemala. Most try again. The luckiest make it to the United States in a month. Others, who stop to work along the way, take a year or longer.

Like many others, Enrique has made several attempts. Six months ago, the first time he set out to find Lourdes, he was still a naïve kid. Now he is a veteran of the treacherous journey through Mexico.

Setting out with his friend José was the first attempt. It was more like a trial run for what was to come. It was then that *la migra* captured them on top of a train and sent them back to Central America on the Bus of Tears.

The second attempt: Enrique journeyed by himself. Five days and 150 miles into Mexico, he made the mistake of falling asleep on top of a train with his shoes off. Police stopped the train near the town of Tonalá to hunt for migrants, and Enrique had to jump off. Barefoot, he could not run far. He hid overnight in some grass, then was captured and put on the bus back to Guatemala.

The third: After two days, police surprised him while he was asleep in an empty house near Chahuites, 190 miles into Mexico. They robbed him, he says, and then turned him over to *la migra,* who put him, once more, on the bus to Guatemala.

The fourth: After a day and twelve miles, police caught him sleeping on top of a mausoleum in a graveyard near the depot in Tapachula, Mexico. *La migra* took Enrique back to Guatemala.

The fifth: *La migra* captured him as he walked along the tracks in Querétaro, north of Mexico City. Enrique was 838 miles and almost a week into his journey. He had been stung in the face by a swarm of bees. For the fifth time, immigration agents shipped him back to Guatemala.

The sixth: He nearly succeeded. It took him more than five days. He crossed 1,564 miles. He reached the Rio Grande and actually saw the United States. He was eating alone near some railroad tracks when *migra* agents grabbed him. They sent him to a detention center called *el Corralón,* the Corral, in Mexico City. The next day they bused him for fourteen hours, all the way back to Guatemala. A sign in block letters on top of a hill says BIENVENIDOS A GUATEMALA.

It was as if he had never left.

Some migrants realize, sitting on the bus, that they can take no more. They slump in their seats, tearful, weak, and sometimes penniless. Often something tragic has broken their willpower: a violent assault, a rape, or a fall from a train. They no longer believe it's possible to reach America. Others have been on the bus dozens of times, but they vow to keep trying, no matter what. They plot how they will try again, using the knowledge they have gained from previous attempts. On his sixth ride back to Guatemala, Enrique's exhaustion tempts him to give up, but he thinks of his mother.

It is on his seventh attempt that he suffers the injuries that leave him destitute in Las Anonas.

Here is what Enrique recalls:

It is night. He is riding on a freight train. A stranger climbs up the side of his tanker car and asks for a cigarette. The man moves quickly, but Enrique is not alarmed. Sometimes migrants riding on the train climb from car to car trying to move forward or backward.

Trees hide the light of the moon, and Enrique does not see two men who are behind the stranger, or three more creeping up the other side of the car. Dozens of migrants cling to the train, but no one is within shouting distance.

One of the men reaches Enrique and grabs him with both hands. Someone else seizes him from behind. They slam him facedown. All six surround him. Take off everything, one says. Another swings a wooden club. It cracks into the back of Enrique's head, then smacks his face.

Enrique feels someone yank off his shoes. Hands paw through his pockets. One of the men pulls out a small scrap of paper. It has his mother's telephone number. Without it, he has no way to locate her. The man tosses the paper into the air. Enrique sees it flutter away.

The men pull off his pants. His mother's number is inked inside the waistband. Enrique has less than fifty pesos in the pockets, only a few coins that he has gathered begging. The men curse and fling the pants overboard.

The blows land harder.

"Don't kill me," Enrique pleads.

"Shut up!" someone says.

Enrique's cap flies away. Someone rips off his shirt. Another blow hits the left side of his face. It shatters three teeth. They rattle like broken glass in his mouth. The men pummel him for what seems like ten minutes. The robbery has turned into blood sport.

One of the men stands over Enrique, straddling him. He wraps the sleeve of a jacket around Enrique's neck and starts to twist.

Enrique wheezes, coughs, and gasps for air. His hands move feverishly from his neck to his face as he tries to breathe and protect his face from the blows.

"Throw him off the train," one man yells.

Enrique's mind races to his mother. He will be buried in an unmarked grave, and she will never know what happened. Please, he asks God, don't let me die without seeing her again.

The man with the jacket slips. The noose around Enrique's neck loosens.

Enrique struggles to his knees, ready to run. He has been stripped of everything but his underwear. He manages to stand. He runs along the top of the fuel car, desperately trying to balance on the smooth, curved surface. Loose tracks flail the train from side to side. There are no lights. It is so dark he can barely see his feet. The train is rolling at what must be forty miles per hour. Leaping from one car to another at such speed would be suicidal. Enrique knows he could slip, fall between the cars, and be sucked under.

He stumbles, then regains his footing. In half a dozen strides, he reaches the rear of the car.

He hears the men coming. Carefully, he jumps down onto the coupler that holds the cars together. It is just inches from the hot, churning wheels. He hears the muffled pop of gunshots and knows what he must do. He leaps from the train, flinging himself outward into the black void.

He hits dirt by the tracks and crumples to the ground. He crawls thirty feet. His knees throb. Finally, he collapses under a small mango tree.

Enrique cannot see blood, but he senses it everywhere. It runs in gooey dribbles down his face and out of his ears and nose. It tastes bitter in his mouth. Still, he feels overwhelming relief: the blows have stopped.

Enrique sleeps for maybe twelve hours, then stirs and tries to sit. The sun is high and hot. Enrique's left eyelid won't open. He can't see very well. His battered knees don't want to bend.

He grabs a stick and pulls himself up. Slowly, barefoot and with swollen knees, he hobbles north alongside the rails. He sees a rancher and asks for water. Get lost, the rancher says. Enrique grows dizzy and confused. He walks the other way, south along the tracks. After what seems to be several hours, he is back where he began, at the mango tree.

Just beyond it is a thatched hut surrounded by a white fence. It belongs to field hand Sirenio Gómez Fuentes, who watches as the bloodied boy stumbles toward him.

GOOD MEDICINE

Mayor Díaz's driver rushes Enrique to San Pedro Tapanatepec, to the last medical clinic still open in the area that night.

At the one-room clinic, Dr. Guillermo Toledo Montes huddles over Enrique, who is lying on a stainless steel table. He examines the boy's injuries. Enrique's left eye socket has a severe concussion. The eyelid is injured and may droop forever. His back is covered with bruises and he has several deep gouges on his right leg. Hidden under his hair is an open wound. Two of his top teeth are broken. So is one on the bottom.

Dr. Toledo jabs a needle with local anesthetic under the skin near Enrique's eye, then into his forehead. He scrubs dirt out of the wounds and thinks of the migrants he has treated who have died.

Many have fallen off a train or, like Enrique, been beaten up by bandits or gangsters. Some have been shot. Injured migrants who cannot move sometimes have to wait one or two days until someone finally walks by, discovers them, and stops to help.

Sometimes the ambulance workers must pry a flattened hand or leg off the rails to move the migrant. Other times, the migrant is dead by the time they arrive. Ambulance workers aren't supposed to transport dead people. Still, sometimes, they take the body away, so vultures won't eat it.

Some migrants who have lost an arm, a leg, or a foot are too ashamed to go back home and show their families what has become of them. Social workers say to the migrants who return: tell other people there not to travel this way.

"You should give thanks you are alive," the doctor says to Enrique. "Why don't you go home?"

"No." Enrique shakes his head. "I have to go north."

Politely, Enrique asks if there is a way that he can pay for his care, as well as for the antibiotics and the anti-inflammatory drugs. The doctor shakes his head. He knows Enrique cannot pay for the treatment.

At dawn, Enrique leaves, hoping to catch a bus back to the railroad tracks. People stare at his injured face. Without a word, one man hands him fifty pesos. Another gives him twenty. He limps on, heading for the outskirts of town.

The pain is too great, so he flags down a car. "Will you give me a ride?"

"Get in," the driver says.

Enrique does. It is a costly mistake. The driver is an off-duty immigration officer. He pulls into a *migra* checkpoint and turns Enrique over. You can't keep going north, the agents say.

Next time, he prays, he will make it.

He is ushered onto yet another bus, with its smell of sweat and diesel fumes, back to the Guatemalan border. He is relieved that there are no Central American gangsters on board this time. Sometimes they let themselves be caught by *la migra* so they can beat and rob the migrants on the buses. They move from seat to seat, threatening the passengers with ice picks and demanding everything they have.

The twenty other migrants on Enrique's bus are depressed. They talk of giving up. For long stretches, the bus is quiet, save for the rattle of the muffler.

In spite of everything, Enrique has failed again—he will not reach the United States this time, either. He glares out the window of the Bus of Tears. Seven times! All his effort, money, and time. When will he make it over the border to his mother? He tells himself over and over that he'll just have to try again.

4

FACING THE BEAST

Enrique wades chest-deep across the Río Suchiate. The river forms a border. Behind him is Guatemala. Before him is Mexico's southernmost state, Chiapas. "*Ahora nos enfrentamos a la bestia.* Now we face the beast," migrants say when they enter Chiapas. Enrique will risk "the beast" again because he needs to find his mother.

This is his eighth attempt to reach *el Norte*.

The water is the color of coffee with too much cream. Each time he crosses, as the rainy season approaches, the river is higher and higher. He is stoop-shouldered and cannot swim. The logo on his cap boasts hollowly, NO FEAR. He always crosses with one or two other migrants, in case he slips and starts to drown. Chin high, he staggers across, stumbling on the uneven riverbed, straining against the current. Exhausted, he reaches the far bank.

Enrique has discovered several important things about the state of Chiapas:

In Chiapas, do not take buses. Buses pass through nine permanent immigration checkpoints. Trains pass through checkpoints as well, but Enrique can jump off a train as it brakes. Inside a bus, he would be stuck.

In Chiapas, never ride trains alone. The best time to move forward is at night or when there is fog. Then he can see immigration agents' flashlights but the agents cannot see him.

In Chiapas, do not trust anyone. Residents tend to dislike migrants. Even the authorities, including police and immigration agents, are corrupt and may rob or rape you.

With Central America safely behind him, Enrique sneaks into a cemetery to rest. In the cemetery he is close enough to the tracks to hear a train coming, its diesel engine growling and its horns blaring, but far enough away to avoid police who might be hovering around the station looking for migrants. Enrique hopes there will be a train tomorrow. Missing one means waiting two or three days for the next train.

He washes his mouth with urine, a home remedy for his aching, broken teeth. He stuffs a few rags under his head for a pillow and slips into sleep.

Sleeping among the dead is eerily calming. The cemetery is beautiful in the light of the yellow moon. The sky is midnight blue. Enrique can see stars around the ceiba trees that shroud the headstones. Crosses and crypts are painted periwinkle, neon green, and purple. A wind touches the tree branches and the leaves flutter and murmur in the gathering light. A bigger gust moves the vast branches, commanding them to dance.

The same darkness and isolation that give the graveyard beauty also make it a place of great peril. There have been many harrowing atrocities in these dark spaces, between the tombstones, worst of all rape and murder. A young woman was found dead; she had been raped, then beaten with stones.

"Wake up." The warning is only a whisper, but Enrique hears it. The words are from the boy who was sleeping next to him.

It is just before dawn. Five pickup trucks filled with police coast up to the cemetery, their lights out. Cops are striding through the maze of pathways, fanning out among the graves, armed with rifles, shotguns, and pistols. Enrique hears migrants trying to run, stampeding among the graves, but he knows there is no point. Weeks ago he tried to flee from police in this very cemetery. He was caught and deported.

Trying not to breathe, he flattens himself on the mausoleum roof where he was sleeping. A policeman peers up over the edge of the crypt and straight at him.

There is no escape.

Enrique and the other migrants are marched off to the Tapachula jail.

"Name?" "Age?" "Where are you from?" the policemen bark, taking notes.

The migrants are led into an enclosed patio. They wait

anxiously. Soon they will be shoved into a packed jail cell, then deported. As they mill about, a rumor starts going around: a train headed north is leaving at ten a.m.

I *can't* miss it, Enrique says to himself. Urgently, he looks around. How can he escape? Walls surround the patio, and *migra* agents are standing nearby.

Enrique sees an old bicycle leaning against the wall. Now he watches *la migra* carefully. For a moment they look distracted; he climbs on top of the bicycle. Other migrants hoist him higher. He grabs a water pipe and pulls himself over the wall and onto the roof of an adjoining house. He jumps, and the soles of his feet smack onto the ground. His head pounds; it is still swollen from being battered.

But he is free.

Before *la migra* can notice, Enrique runs back toward the cemetery to hide until ten a.m. At the first rumble of the departing train, the cemetery comes to life as dozens of migrants, children among them, appear from behind the bushes, trees, and tombs where they have been hiding.

On this day, March 26, 2000, Enrique is among them.

Two days ago he was battered in Las Anonas; yesterday he was shuttled back to Guatemala on the deportation bus. Now he and the other migrants run on trails between the graves and dash headlong down a hill. A sewage canal, twenty feet wide, separates them from the train rails. They cross the canal on seven stones, jumping from one to another over a nauseating stream of black water. They gather on the other side, shaking the dampness from their feet. Now they are only yards from the rails.

Enrique sprints alongside rolling freight cars, focusing on his footing. The roadbed is slanted at a forty-five-degree angle and scattered with rocks as big as his fist. It is hard to keep his balance in his tattered sneakers.

Here the locomotives accelerate, sometimes reaching twenty-five miles per hour. He knows he needs to be speedy and climb up the ladder before the train reaches a bridge just beyond the cemetery. If he runs too slowly, when he tries to climb up, the ladder will yank him forward and send him sprawling. Then the churning wheels could take an arm, a leg, perhaps his life.

"*Se lo comió el tren.* The train ate him up," other migrants will say.

Already Enrique has four jagged scars on his shins from frenzied efforts to board trains.

The lowest rung of the ladder is waist-high. When the train leans away, it is higher. If the train hits a curve, the wheels kick up hot white sparks, burning Enrique's skin. By this time around, he has learned that if he overthinks all of this too long, he will fall behind—and the train will pass him by. Enrique grabs one of its ladders, summons his strength, and pulls himself up.

He is aboard.

Enrique looks ahead on the train. Men and boys are hanging on to the sides of tank cars, trying to find a spot to sit or stand.

Suddenly Enrique hears screams. Three cars away, a boy, twelve or thirteen years old, has managed to grab the bottom rung of a ladder on a fuel tanker, but he cannot haul himself up. Air rushing beneath the train is sucking his legs under the car. It is tugging at him harder, drawing his feet toward the wheels.

"Pull yourself up!" a man calls.

"Don't let go!" another man shouts. He and others crawl along the top of the train to a nearby car. They hope to reach the boy's car before he is so exhausted he must let go. By then, his tired arms would have little strength left to push away from the train's wheels.

Enrique gasps as the boy dangles from the ladder. The boy is struggling to keep his grip. Carefully, men crawl down and reach for him. They lift him up slowly. The rungs batter his legs, but he is alive. He still has his feet.

DANGER

There are few women on board the train today; it is too dangerous.

A University of Houston study found that nearly one in six migrant girls detained by authorities in Texas say they have been sexually assaulted during their journey. Many female migrants are gang-raped. One of them was a Salvadoran woman, four months pregnant, who was assaulted at gunpoint by thirteen bandits along the railroad tracks to the south. The rape victims arrive at hospitals with severe internal bleeding and long scratch marks on their bodies. Some get pregnant. A few go mad. In one Chiapas shelter, one raped woman paces, her arms tightly crossed in front of her, a blank stare on her face. At another shelter, a woman spends hours each day in the shower, trying to cleanse herself of the attack.

Some girls journeying north cut off their hair, bind their breasts, and try to pass for boys. Others scrawl on their chests *Tengo SIDA,* "I have AIDS," to scare men off. Men are also targets of rape and sexual assault. Rape is one way Mexicans demean and humiliate Central Americans, who are sometimes seen as inferior because they come from less developed countries, says Olivia Ruiz, a cultural anthropologist at El Colegio de la Frontera Norte in Tijuana.

THE IRON HORSE

Migrants hang on to the sides of cars, trying to find a spot to perch. Enrique guesses there are more than two hundred on board, a small army of them who charged out of the cemetery with nothing but their cunning. They wage what a priest at a migrant shelter calls *la guerra sin nombre,* the war with no name. Chiapas, he says, is "a cemetery with no crosses, where people die without even getting a prayer." A human rights report said that migrants trying to make it through Chiapas face "an authentic race against time and death."

Enrique considers carefully. Which car will he ride on? This time he will be more cautious about being seen.

He could lie flat on the roof of a boxcar and hide. But boxcars have little on top to hold on to. Inside the boxcar might be better, but what if someone locked the door, trapping him? It could turn into an oven.

Enrique looks elsewhere. A good place to hide could be under the cars, balancing on a small shock absorber, but he might be too big to fit. Besides, trains kick up rocks. Worse, if his arms grew tired or if he fell asleep, he would drop directly under the wheels. He tells himself: That's crazy.

He could stand on a tiny ledge, barely big enough for his feet, on the end of a hopper car. Or he could sit on the round compressor at the end of some hoppers, his feet dangling just above the train wheels: shiny metal, three feet in diameter, five inches thick, churning. His hands would turn numb after hours of hanging on, though.

Enrique settles for the top of a hopper. From his perch fourteen feet up, he can see anyone approaching on either side of the tracks up ahead or from another car. As usual, the train lurches hard from side to side. Enrique holds on with both hands.

He doesn't carry anything that might keep him from running fast. At most, a plastic bottle for water, tied to his arm. Some migrants climb on board with a toothbrush tucked into a pocket. A few allow themselves a small reminder of family. Maybe a rosary, or a Bible, or a tiny drawing of San Cristóbal, the patron saint of travelers, or of San Judas Tadeo, the patron saint of desperate situations. One father wraps his eight-year-old daughter's favorite hair band around his wrist.

There are several children on board, and Grupo Beta, the government migrant rights group in Chiapas, estimates that

20 to 30 percent of migrants who board here are fifteen or younger. Enrique has encountered kids as young as nine. Some speak only with big brown eyes or a shy smile. Others talk openly about their mothers: "I felt alone. I only talked to her on the phone. I didn't like that. I want to see her. When I see her, I'm going to hug her a lot, with everything I have."

Enrique nods understandingly as they speak. He confides in them, too. They share the burden of their loneliness. Although Enrique's efforts to survive often force thoughts of his mother out of his mind, at times he thinks of her with a longing that is overwhelming. He remembers when she would call Honduras from the United States, the concern in her voice, how she would not hang up before saying, "I love you. I miss you."

Wheels rumble, screech, and clang. The train speeds up and slows down unpredictably, tossing the travelers backward and forward. Sometimes each car rocks the other way from the ones ahead and behind. Migrants call the train *El Gusano de Hierro,* The Iron Worm, for how it squirms up the tracks. In Chiapas, the tracks are twenty years old. Some of the ties sink, especially during the rainy season, when the roadbed turns soggy and soft. Grass grows on the rails, making them slippery. When the cars round a bend, they feel as if they might overturn. Derailments are common. The train Enrique is on runs only a few times a week, but it derails three times a month, on average—with seventeen accidents in a particularly bad month—by the count of Jorge Reinoso, the railroad's chief of operations in Chiapas. One year before, a hopper car like Enrique's overturned with a load of sand, burying three migrants alive. In another spot, six hoppers tumbled over. The cars' rusty remains lie scattered, upside down, next to the tracks.

Enrique was once on a train that derailed. His car lurched so violently that he briefly thought of jumping off to save himself. Enrique rarely lets himself admit to being afraid, but he is scared that his car might tip. He holds on with both hands.

In spite of his fear, Enrique is struck by the magic of the train—its power and speed, and, above all, its ability to take him to his mother. To Enrique, it is *El Caballo de Hierro,* The Iron Horse.

Other migrants believe the train has a noble purpose. Sometimes the train tops are packed with migrants, all facing north, toward a new land. *El Tren Peregrino,* they call it. The Pilgrim's Train.

The train picks up speed. It passes a brown river that smells of sewage. A dark form emerges ahead. Migrants at the front of the train call back a warning over the train's deafening din. They sound an alarm, migrant to migrant, car to car. *"¡Rama!"* the migrants yell. "Branch!" The train is hurtling toward a thick canopy of tree branches.

Enrique and the other riders sway in unison, ducking the same branches—left, then right. One moment of carelessness—a glance down at a watch, a look toward the back of the train at the wrong moment—and the branches will hurl them into the air.

A DREADED STOP

Each time the train slows, Enrique goes on high alert for *la migra*. Migrants wake one another and begin climbing down to prepare to jump. They lean outward, trying to glimpse what is causing the train to change pace. Is it another false alarm? A bad curve, a migrant disconnecting the brake line, or a conductor pulling off onto a siding to let another train pass can all cause a train to slow. If the train speeds up again, everyone climbs back up. The movement down and up the ladders looks almost choreographed.

Slowing down at Huixtla, with its red-and-yellow depot, can mean only one thing: La Arrocera is coming up. La Arrocera is the immigration checkpoint Enrique fears most. It is in an isolated agricultural area, with few houses or busy streets where migrants can hide. Usually half of those aboard a train here are caught by *migra* agents. Enrique decides he will jump off the train, run around the checkpoint, and catch up with the train so he can reboard it on the other side.

He arrives in the heat of noon. Tension builds. Some migrants stand on top of the train to see if *migra* agents are up ahead. The first migrants who spot agents down the tracks scream a warning to the others: "*¡Bájense!* Get down!" As the train brakes, migrants jump.

The train stops. Enrique lies flat, facedown, arms spread-eagle, hoping *la migra* won't see him. But several agents do. Sometimes Mexican immigration authorities put people on the train who pretend to be migrants. The imposters radio ahead to tell agents where migrants are hidden and how many are on each train.

Enrique scrambles to his feet and races along the top of the train, soaring across the four-foot gaps between cars. As he runs, three agents run alongside him on the ground, pelting him with rocks and sticks. Stones clang against the metal.

"*¡Alto! ¡Alto!* Stop! Stop!" the agents holler.

There is no ladder all the way to the top. The only way agents can reach him is to straddle their legs across two adjoining boxcars, using the horizontal ridges on the ends of the car to inch higher. Maybe they won't come up after him.

"*¡Bájate!* Get down!" they shout. They curse him.

"No! I'm not coming down!" he shouts back.

The agents summon reinforcements. One starts to climb, shimmying up the side of the boxcar.

Enrique flees from car to car, more than twenty cars in all, struggling to keep his footing each time he leaps from a hopper to a fuel tanker, which is lower and has a rounded top. He is running out of train to stand on. He will have to jump off and go around the La Arrocera checkpoint on foot, alone. It may be suicidal, but he has no choice. More stones fly through the air. They miss him and bounce off the train with a *ping*. Enrique scurries down a ladder and sprints into the bushes.

As Enrique runs, he hears what he thinks are gunshots behind him. Mexican immigration agents are prohibited from carrying firearms. According to a retired agent, however, most ignore the rule and carry pistols anyway. Workers at a local migrant shelter tell of migrants who have been hit by bullets. Others tell of torture. Enrique once met a man whose chest was scarred with cigarette burns. The man told him that a *migra* agent at La Arrocera branded him.

In the brush, though, Enrique worries less about agents than about what awaits him in the woods. Swarms of bandits, some carrying Uzis, some on drugs, patrol this three-mile dirt path he will have to use to go around La Arrocera. Whereas gangsters rule on the train tops, bandits stay in isolated areas like this. Human rights activists and some police agencies say these bandits commit some of the worst atrocities—rapes and torture. They split what they steal from their victims with the police, who allow them to operate freely.

Migrants hide their money in case they are caught by robbers. Some stitch it into the seams of their pants. Others put a bit in their shoes, a bit in their shirts, or a few coins in their mouths. Still others tuck money into their underwear. Others hollow out mangoes, drop their pesos inside, then pretend to be eating the fruit.

Enrique figures he doesn't have enough money to bother hiding it. He knows bandits catch on to these hiding places, anyway: they split open waistbands, collars, and cuffs looking for money. Local residents see groups of migrants walking down dirt roads naked, stripped of everything, just as Enrique had been, back in Las Anonas.

Migrants who fight back are beaten—or worse. The bandits warn: If you say anything to the authorities, we will find you and kill you.

The police force itself is involved in crime and cannot be relied on for help. Many of the bandits are current or former police officers, says Grupo Beta Sur supervisor Mario Campos Gutiérrez. If these bandits are arrested, they pay bribes to police headquarters and are quickly released without any consequences. Witness statements against them mysteriously "disappear."

For migrants, going to police authorities would be dangerous anyway because they could be deported. Because migrants are on the run, they cannot wait around for months until a trial to testify against the bandits. This makes them ideal victims for robbers to attack.

Migrants have asked members of Grupo Beta Sur why the authorities don't clamp down on the gangsters. Grupo Beta Sur agents told them they needed witnesses. They urged the migrants to step forward and report abuses. One teenager who did was brutally beaten by Mara Salvatrucha gangsters later that day.

And bandits long ago intimidated any La Arrocera residents who considered testifying.

"If you say anything, they kill you. Better to keep your mouth shut," says a local elderly man, who is afraid to give his full name. An ice cream vendor near La Arrocera adds, "If you turn them in, they get out, and they come after you. They operate by light of day. There is no law here."

The last time Enrique sneaked past La Arrocera, he was lucky because he was careful. He stuck with a band of street gangsters. Bandits try to avoid gangsters, who are likely to be armed. They prefer to attack someone who can't shoot back. Enrique and the gangsters ran past a group of Mexican men standing by the tracks, machetes at their sides. The men looked at them intently but did not move or attack.

This time, Enrique is alone. He focuses on the thought that will make him run the fastest: I cannot miss the train. If he misses the one he just left, he knows he will be waiting for days in the bushes and tall grass until another one comes.

Enrique races so fast he feels the blood pounding at his temples. Long, wet grass coils around his feet. He stumbles but never stops running.

Enrique crawls under a barbed-wire fence, then under a double strand of smooth wire. It is electrified. At night, locals who live along the train tracks hear the piercing screams of migrants who have been electrocuted by this wire. "Help me! Help me!" they wail. These locals have also found train riders who have lost arms, legs, or heads along the tracks, migrants who were injured as they tried to outrun the agents and get onto and off of moving trains.

He reaches the Cuil bridge, which spans a stream of murky brown water. The bridge, migrants and Grupo Beta Sur officers say, is the most dangerous spot. Bandits hide in trees, waiting to pounce on migrants. They use children as lookouts; in exchange for a coin or a piece of candy, the children race ahead on their bicycles to tell the bandits when migrants are drawing near. As migrants near the bridge, the bandits drop down and surround them. Other robbers hide along the tracks on the bridge and below it—an area thick with bushes and vines. One bandit fishes in the river or cuts grass with a machete, like a fieldworker, and whistles to the others to set a trap.

Enrique dashes across the bridge and keeps his pace. If there are bandits in the distance, he does not notice them. Mountains stand to his right. The ground is so wet that farmers grow rice between their rows of corn. He can feel humidity rising from the loamy earth. It saps his energy, but he runs on.

Finally, he stops, doubled over, panting.

He is not sure why, but he has survived La Arrocera. Maybe it was his extra caution; maybe it was that he never stopped running; maybe it was his decision to hide atop the boxcar instead of jumping off immediately, which meant that bandits targeted migrants ahead of him.

He is desperate for water. He spots a house.

The people inside are not likely to give him any. The people of Chiapas are fed up with Central American migrants. Central Americans are poorer than Mexicans, and here they are seen as backward and ignorant. People think they bring disease, prostitution, and crime and take away jobs. They tell of a man from Chiapas who sold chickens in a market and was kind to outsiders. He gave three Salvadorans a place to sleep, and work slaughtering and plucking birds. The Salvadorans robbed and killed him.

Migrants like Enrique are called "stinking undocumented." They are cursed, taunted. Dogs are set upon them. Barefoot children throw rocks at them. Some use slingshots and shout, "Go to work!" and "Get out! Get out!"

Drinking water can be impossible to come by. Migrants filter ditch sewage through T-shirts. Finding food can be just as difficult. Enrique is counting: in some places, people at seven of every ten houses turn him away.

"No," they say, "we haven't cooked today. We don't have any tortillas. Try somewhere else." They press the door closed in his face.

Many La Arrocera residents lock themselves inside their homes when they hear the train coming. Sometimes it is worse: people in the houses turn the migrants in.

Enrique sees another migrant who has managed to make it around La Arrocera. He, too, needs water badly, but he doesn't dare ask. To migrants, begging in Chiapas is like walking up to a loaded gun.

"I'll go," Enrique says. "If they catch someone, it will be me."

Enrique also knows he is less likely to frighten people if he begs alone.

Enrique approaches a house and speaks softly, his head slightly bowed. "I'm hungry. Can you spare a taco? Some water?" The woman inside sees injuries from the train-top beating he took during his last attempt to go north. She gives him water, bread, and beans. The other migrant comes nearer. She gives him food, too.

A horn blows. Enrique runs to the tracks. He looks all around, trying to spot *migra* agents, who sometimes race ahead in their trucks to catch migrants as they reboard. Other migrants who have survived La Arrocera come out of the bushes. They sprint alongside the train and reach for the ladders on the freight cars.

Sometimes train drivers back up the locomotive and get a running start. They accelerate to prevent migrants from reboarding up ahead. This time, though, the train isn't going full throttle.

Enrique climbs up onto a hopper. The train picks up speed. For the moment, he relaxes.

WAITING IN HONDURAS

Meanwhile, Enrique's girlfriend, María Isabel, is sure Enrique hasn't really left Honduras. This is all a joke, she thinks. He has probably gone to visit a friend. He'll be back any day.

A couple of weeks after he disappears, María Isabel realizes it is no joke.

María Isabel knows Enrique longed to be with his mother. He spoke often of going north to be with Lourdes. Still, how could he leave her? What if he is harmed or killed crossing Mexico? What if she never sees him again?

Tearfully, she prays he will be caught and deported back to Honduras, back by her side.

She doesn't feel well and loses weight. She quits night school. What if she *is* pregnant and Enrique dies trying to make it to his mother? Then she will be alone, raising their child.

She makes a plan to follow Enrique north, to find him in Mexico or in the United States. But she has no money. She fears being assaulted or raped. Her family scolds her. "Are you crazy? You want to die along the way?" If you are pregnant, they tell her, you could lose the child on the road.

María Isabel listens in silence. She knows they are right. All she can do now is wait.

HEAT WAVES

The Iron Worm squeaks, groans, and clanks its way north. Enrique eyes the scenery over the edge of the hopper car he is riding. Off to the right are hillsides covered with coffee plants. Cornstalks grow up against the rails. The train moves through a sea of plantain trees, lush and tropical.

By early afternoon, it is 105 degrees. The sun reflects off the metal of the train, stinging Enrique's eyes, draining the little energy he has left. His head still throbs. His skin tingles as he breaks into a full-bodied sweat. He moves around on the car, chasing patches of shade. Finally, he strips off his shirt and sits on it. The locomotive blows warm diesel smoke. People burn trash by the rails, sending up more heat and a searing stench. Many of the migrants aboard have had their caps stolen, so they wrap their heads in T-shirts. They gaze enviously at villagers cooling themselves in streams and washing off after a day of fieldwork, and at others who doze in hammocks slung in shady spots near adobe and cinder-block homes. The train cars sway from side to side, up and down like bobbing ice cubes.

Enrique's palms burn when he holds on to the hopper. He risks riding no-hands. He cannot let himself fall asleep; one good shake of the train and he would tumble off. Other migrants have taught him tricks on how to stay awake.

Slap your own face, they say, do squats, pour drops of alcohol into your eyes, sing—do anything to keep yourself from getting tired. At four a.m. the train sounds like a chorus.

Mara Salvatrucha street gangsters always prowl the train tops in Chiapas, in groups of ten or twenty, looking for sleepers. Many gangsters settle in Chiapas after committing crimes in the United States and being deported to their home countries in Central America. Gangsters say the police target and kill them in Central America, so they've settled in Mexico and made a good business robbing migrants on top of the trains. Before a train leaves, they try to figure out which migrants are the best targets, which ones have money or food, and which ones are weakest. They try to get friendly with the migrants, telling them they have already done the train ride. Maybe they can offer tips? Enrique knows to watch for anyone with tattoos, especially gangsters who have skulls inked around their ankles—one skull, some say, for every person they have killed. Some wear black knit hats they can pull down over their faces.

Their brutality is legendary. Often they are high on marijuana or crack cocaine. Drugs embolden them. They are armed with machetes, knives, bats, and pistols. When the train gains speed, they surround a group of migrants. They tell them: Hand over your money or die. A train engineer, Emilio Canteros Méndez, often sees the armed gangs through his rearview mirror. Fights erupt on top of the boxcars. Migrants who anger the gangsters because they don't have money or resist are regularly tossed off moving trains or left dead on top of the cars, to be discovered by train workers at the next stop.

Enrique has heard of the two most dangerous gangsters: El Indio, who claims the Guatemalan side of the Mexican border, and Blackie, a chubby Salvadoran with dark skin and MS tattooed on his forehead, whose territory stretches from the border to Arriaga in northern Chiapas.

During one of his first attempts to go north, a chance meeting saved Enrique from the worst of the gangs. As he set out on his trip, he noticed another teenager, a gangster named El Brujo, at the bus station in Honduras waiting to go to the Mexican border. Enrique doesn't like gangs. But as the two spent hours traveling through Honduras and Guatemala together, he and El Brujo became friends. On their first train ride through Chiapas, El Brujo introduced Enrique to other teenage MS members. There was Big Daddy, a skinny and short teenager, and El Payaso, the Clown, who had a big mouth and eyes. Sticking with these gang members protected him from attacks along the way.

On his seventh trip, the convenient relationship ended. One of the MS gangsters is upset because a member of the rival gang, an 18th Streeter, has stolen his shirt. He decides to throw the 18th Streeter off the train. Enrique refuses to participate, creating a rift.

"If you are MS, you have to kill Eighteenth Streeters. And if you are Eighteenth Street, you must kill MS. I wasn't like that," Enrique says.

After the fight, the gang members stop riding with Enrique.

That night, without their protection, he is beaten by the six men on top of the train.

Now that he is riding alone, he must stay extra alert. He is terrified of another beating. Every time someone new jumps onto his car, he tenses. Fear, he realizes, is a tool he can use to keep himself awake. He climbs on top of the tank car and takes a running leap. With arms spread, as if he were flying, he jumps to one swaying boxcar, then another. Some cars are nine feet apart.

The train passes into northern Chiapas. Enrique sees men with hoes tending their corn and women inside their kitchens patting tortillas into shape. Cowboys ride past and smile, fieldworkers wave their machetes and cheer the migrants on: *"¡Qué bueno!"* Mountains draw closer. Plantain fields soften into cow pastures. Enrique's train slows to a crawl. Monarch butterflies flutter alongside, overtaking his car.

As the sun sets and the oppressive heat breaks, he hears crickets and frogs begin their music and join the migrant chorus. The moon rises. Thousands of fireflies flicker around the train. Stars come out to shine, so many they seem jammed together, brilliant points of light all across the sky.

The train nears San Ramón, close to the northern state line. This is where police stage their biggest shakedowns. But it is past midnight now, and the judicial police are probably asleep.

Mario Campos Gutiérrez, the Grupo Beta Sur supervisor, estimates that half of those who try to migrate north eventually get here—after repeated attempts. Migrants know getting this far means conquering the toughest part of the journey. As one migrant put it, "When I get to this point, I begin to sing hallelujah."

Enrique greets the dawn without incident. The stars recede. The sky lightens behind the mountains to the east, and mist rises off the fields on both sides of the tracks. Men trot by on burros with tin milk containers strapped to their saddles, starting their morning deliveries.

He puts Chiapas behind him. He still has far to go, but he has faced this beast of a state eight times now, and he has lived through it. It is an achievement, and he is proud of it.

DEVOURED

Many migrants who first set out on the train with Enrique have been caught and deported. Others have fared worse; they are left broken by Chiapas. As Enrique slowly recovers from his beating, he hears horror stories from other migrants of riders who are mutilated by the train itself.

The Red Cross estimates that every other day in Chiapas alone, a migrant riding the freight trains loses an arm, leg, hand, or foot. This estimate does not include people who die instantly. One police chief keeps snapshots of the dead in a black book. He keeps the book handy, hoping someone will identify the bodies. No one ever comes to look.

A young Honduran seventeen-year-old, Carlos Roberto Díaz Osorto, lies in bed number 1 of the trauma unit at Hospital Civil in southern Mexico. Four days before he was brought in, Carlos had seen a man get both legs cut off by a freight train. But he had pushed fear out of his mind. He was going to the United States to find work.

Carlos had almost crossed Chiapas. Racing alongside a train, he asked himself: Should I get on or not? His cousins, who were running with him, grabbed on to the sixth car from the end. Carlos panicked. Would he be left behind?

The train came to a bridge. Carlos did not give up. His shoelaces were loose. His left shoe flew off. Then his right shoe. He reached for a ladder on a fuel tanker, but the car was moving too fast, and he let go. He grabbed a railing.

The tanker jerked hard. Carlos held on, but he could feel air rushing beneath the car, sucking his legs in, close to the wheels. His fingers uncurled. He tried to bounce his feet off the wheels and push away. But as he let go, the air pulled him in. The wheels flattened his right foot, then sliced through his left leg above the knee.

"Help me! Help me! It hurts!" he screamed. He began to pant, to sweat, to ask for water, not sure anyone could hear him.

Paramedics from the Mexican Red Cross found him lying by the tracks. He had lost nearly a third of his blood. A doctor cut his bones, then sealed each artery and vein. He stretched skin over the openings and stitched them shut. Sometimes there are no drugs available to stave off infection, but Carlos was lucky. The Red Cross located some penicillin.

Many migrants who lose limbs to the train end up back in Tapachula, a dozen blocks from where they first boarded the train, at the Shelter of Jesus the Good Shepherd. The shelter director, Olga Sánchez Martínez, tries to heal migrants left deeply wounded by the beast.

Olga is a petite middle-aged woman with silky black hair down to her hips, and a simple white rosary strung around her neck. She is always in motion, impatient to find solutions to problems. She nurses the migrants until they can be taken back home.

The injured migrants seethe with anger. They curse God. Why didn't he protect them? Their eyes speak fear. Who will ever marry them like this? How will they ever work again? "Let me die," they say.

She perches on the edge of their hospital beds. She strokes their hair.

"God has a plan for you," she says. "You will learn to live—in a different way."

She tells them her story, how an intestinal disease contracted when she was seven, which went untreated because her family had no money for medicine, led to a life of being gravely ill. At times she was blind, mute. Once, she was in a coma for thirty-eight days. Once, she was down to sixty-six pounds, just skin and bones. Once, when she was working at a tortilla factory, a machine tore off two fingertips. She tells them she tried to slit her wrists. One day her doctor told her she had cancer, and only months to live. What would become of her two small children? She wasn't very religious, but she went to church that day, kneeled, and made a pact with God: Heal me and I will heal others.

She studied the Bible. It told her to help the weak, the hungry.

She began visiting patients at a local hospital. One year later, she saw a thirteen-year-old Salvadoran boy who had lost both legs boarding a train. She walked home in tears. How, she asked God, could you be so cruel? She taught herself, watching doctors, how to dress the migrants' wounds. She began taking migrants who had been kicked out of the hospital into her humble home. In 1999, she opened the four-bedroom migrant shelter in a little former tortilla factory someone lent her.

She confesses it has not been easy. She works for free, from dawn until late at night, seven days a week, to obtain money for food, units of blood, medicine, and prostheses. She raises money selling food in the streets and going from car to car, begging, with a picture of a mutilated migrant she's trying to help. People often tell her that she's crazy to help foreigners who could be robbers or murderers, and that she should help Mexicans instead.

Sometimes she loses her patience with God. She can't always quickly come up with the money to buy the blood or medicine migrants need to fight for their lives. What do you want me to do? she asks God angrily. Some migrants are too battered by the beast to save. A thirteen-year-old girl was raped by the side of the tracks and left with a broken neck and shattered hips. She could not move or talk. Olga buried that girl and thirty-nine others. She tries to buy them each a wooden coffin so they can be lowered into the ground with some dignity. Otherwise, their bodies would be lowered, nameless, into common graves in Tapachula.

But most slowly recuperate under Olga's care. A young man who has lost both feet fears going back to his small town in Honduras, where he won't be able to walk the hilly dirt paths, grow beans or corn or coffee, or play soccer with friends. "You are going to walk again," Olga says, vowing to get him prostheses.

A teenage girl, who lost her right foot, fears her husband will leave her. "Don't cry," Olga soothes her. "God wants people who are useful. You must keep going forward. You have your hands. You must go forward and trust in God."

Each night, when she hears the train whistle, she asks God to protect the migrants from the trains and the assaults.

OAXACA

Enrique reaches Oaxaca, the next state north from Chiapas. He is now 285 miles into Mexico. As his train squeals to a stop around noon, migrants jump down and look for houses where they can beg for water and a bite to eat.

La bestia might be behind them, but most are still afraid. In these small towns, strangers stick out. Migrants are especially easy to spot. They wear dirty clothes and smell bad after days or weeks without bathing. Often they have no socks. Their shoes are battered. They have been bitten by mosquitoes. They look exhausted.

Most of the migrants want to hide in bushes on the grassy

slope by the tracks in case there is a *migra* raid. Two boys standing near Enrique are too frightened to go into town. They offer Enrique twenty pesos and ask him to buy food. If he will bring it back, they will share it with him.

Blending in is critical. If he doesn't look like a local, the police might search him and deport him. Enrique takes off his yellow shirt. It is stained and smelling of diesel smoke. Underneath he wears a white one, which he takes off and then puts back on over the dirty one.

Throughout his journey, he has tried to stay clean by finding bits of cardboard to sleep on. When he gets a bottle of water, he saves a little to wash his arms. If he is near a river or stream, he strips and slips into the water. He begs for clean clothes or scrubs the ones he has been wearing and lays them on the riverbank to dry. Maybe he can pass for someone who lives here. He resolves not to panic if he sees a policeman, and to walk confidently, as if he knows where he is going.

He takes the pesos the two migrant boys have given him and walks down the main street, past a bar, a store, a bank, and a pharmacy. He buys enough food for the three of them and stashes it. Then he stops at a barbershop. His curly hair has grown long. It is an easy tip-off. People here tend to have straighter hair.

He strides purposefully inside.

"*¡Órale, jefe!*" he says, using a phrase Oaxacans favor. "Hey, chief!" He mutes his flat Central American accent and speaks softly and in a singsongy way, like a Oaxacan. He asks the barber for a short crop, military style. He pays with the last of his own money, careful not to call it *pisto,* as they do back home. Up here, *pisto* doesn't mean money, it means alcohol. He is careful not to slip up.

Enrique glances into a store window and sees his reflection. It is the first time he has looked at his face since he was beaten. He recoils from what he sees. Scars and bruises. Black and blue. One eyelid droops.

It stops him.

"They really screwed me up," he mutters.

He was five years old when his mother left him. Now he is almost another person. In the window glass, he sees a battered young man, scrawny and disfigured. He is underweight and his eyes are sunken in, with dark circles of exhaustion.

What Enrique sees angers him. It steels his determination to push northward.

5

GIFTS AND FAITH

From the top of his rolling freight car, Enrique sees a figure of Christ.

In the fields of Veracruz, among farmers and their donkeys piled with sugarcane, rises a mountain. It towers over the train he is riding. At the summit stands a statue of Jesus. It is sixty feet tall, dressed in white, with a pink tunic. The statue stretches out both arms. They reach toward Enrique and others on top of the rolling freight cars.

Some stare silently. Others whisper a prayer.

It is early April 2000. Enrique and his fellow migrants have made it nearly a third of the way up the length of Mexico.

Many migrants thank God for their progress. They pray on top of the train cars, asking God to protect them against bandits, who rob and beat them; police, who shake them down;

and *la migra,* the Mexican immigration authorities, who deport them. They ask him to keep them alive until they reach *el Norte.* In exchange for God's help, they make promises: to never drink another drop of alcohol, to be generous and serve him forever.

They carry small Bibles, wrapped in plastic bags to keep dry when they ford rivers or when it rains. Some pages are especially worn. The one that offers the Twenty-third Psalm, for instance: "Yea, though I walk through the valley of the shadow of death, I will fear no evil: for thou art with me; thy rod and thy staff they comfort me." Some migrants rely on a special prayer, the *Oración a las Tres Divinas Personas*—a prayer to the Holy Trinity. It asks God to help them and to disarm any weapon raised against them. It has seven sentences—short enough to recite in a moment of danger. If they rush the words, God will not mind.

That night Enrique climbs to the top of a boxcar. In the starlight, he sees a man on his knees, bending over his Bible, praying. Enrique climbs back down.

He does not turn to God for help. With all the sins he has committed, Enrique thinks he has no right to ask God for anything.

SMALL BUNDLES

What he receives are gifts.

Night has fallen. As the train passes through a tiny town, it blows its soulful horn. Enrique looks over the side. More than a dozen people, mostly women and children, are rushing out of their houses along the tracks, clutching small bundles.

Some of the migrants grow afraid. What are these people holding? Will they throw rocks? The migrants lie low on top of the train. Enrique sees a woman and a boy run up alongside his car.

"¡*Órale, chavo!* Here, boy!" they shout. They toss up a roll of crackers.

Enrique reaches out to grab with one hand but holds tightly to the car with the other. The roll of crackers flies several feet away, bounces off the car, and thumps to the ground.

Now women and children on both sides of the tracks are throwing bundles to the migrants on top of the cars. They run quickly and aim carefully, trying hard not to miss.

Enrique looks down. There, below him, are the same woman and boy from before. They are heaving a blue plastic bag. This time the bundle lands squarely in his arms. It is the first gift. "¡*Gracias!* ¡*Adiós!*" he calls into the darkness. He isn't sure the strangers, who pass by in a flash, even heard him.

He opens the bag. Inside are half a dozen rolls of bread.

Enrique is stunned by the generosity.

Riding trains through the state of Chiapas has taught him to expect the worst from people. But farther north, in the states of Oaxaca and Veracruz, he discovers that people are friendly. In many places throughout Veracruz, people give. Sometimes twenty or thirty people stream out of their homes along the rails and toward the train. They wave. They smile, they shout, and then they throw food. They signal if hostile police are ahead. Perhaps not everyone is that way, but there is a widespread spirit of generosity. Many say it is rooted in residents' indigenous Zapotec and Mixtec cultures.

Besides, some say, giving to migrants is a good way to protest Mexico's policies against illegal immigration. As one man who lives near the tracks in Veracruz puts it, "It's wrong for our government to send people back to Central America. If we don't want to be stopped from going into the United States, how can we stop Central Americans in our country?"

The towns of El Encinar, Fortín de las Flores, Cuichapa, and Presidio in particular are known for their kindness. People living along the tracks are annoyed when migrants take clothing from their laundry lines, a police chief says—but only if they don't ask first. Nightly, neighbors come out to chat after long hours of work as bricklayers and field hands. As the evening cools, they hear a diesel horn.

The train approaches.

Migrants watch from atop the cars as a baker, his hands coated with flour, throws his extra loaves. A seamstress throws sandwiches. A carpenter throws bean burritos. A teenager throws oranges in November, when they are plentiful, and watermelons and pineapples in July. People who have watched migrants fall off the train from exhaustion bring jugs filled with coffee.

A stooped woman, more than a hundred years old, who in her youth was reduced to eating the bark of her plantain tree during the Mexican Revolution, forces her knotted hands to fill bags with tortillas, beans, and salsa so her daughter, who is seventy years old, can run down a rocky slope and heave them onto a train. "If I have one tortilla, I give half away," the stooped woman says. "I know God will bring me more."

Gladys González Hernández waits for the diesel horn. There it is, at last! The girl runs down the narrow aisles of her father's grocery, snatching crackers, water bottles, and pastries off the shelves. She dashes outside. Gladys and her father, Ciro González Ramos, wave to the migrants on board the train. She is six years old.

Ciro González, thirty-five, taught Gladys to do this; he wants her to grow up right.

"Why do you give them food?" she asked him once. Her father said, "Because they have traveled far and haven't eaten."

Down the tracks, another man grabs sweaters from his home, hand-me-downs from relatives. He ties them into a knot, so they will be easier for train riders to catch. His sister ladles lemonade into a plastic bottle, spilling some in her haste. They are running toward the train as the horn on the locomotive grows louder, more frequent.

It is dusk; headlights glow on the train. The ground rumbles. Wheels pound. The brother and sister edge close to the tracks, dig in their heels, and brace each other. The man spots migrants and waves a sweater above his head.

A teenager in a green-and-white shirt edges down the ladder on the hopper. He holds on with his right hand and reaches out with his left.

Now each second counts. The man and woman thrust up the food, drinks, and clothing. The youngster grabs everything.

"*¡Gracias!*" the migrant boy yells above the din.

"*¡Que Dios los lleve!* May God watch over you!" the man and woman shout back, eyes smiling.

These are unlikely places for people to be giving food to strangers. Here, in these rural areas, 30 percent of children five years old and younger eat so little that their growth is stunted. The people who live in humble houses near the rails are often the poorest.

No one recalls when the gift giving started, probably in the 1980s, when Central Americans, fleeing war and poverty, began riding the rails north in large numbers. Eventually people along the tracks, particularly in the state of Veracruz, began to bring food, water, or even just prayers out to the trains, often where they slowed for curves or bad tracks. As the number of migrants has grown, so has the determination to help.

Many people in the area who give are from small towns where roughly one in five youngsters has left for the United States. In these places, residents understand that poor people leave their country because they feel they have to, not because they want to. They have watched and worried as their own children struggled to reach the United States. They know it is even harder, and farther, for the Central Americans to make it.

"I don't like to feel that I have eaten and they haven't," one of the food throwers says.

Another adds: "I figure when I die, I can't take anything with me. So why not give?"

Still others say: "When you see these people, it moves you. It moves you. Can you imagine how far they've come?"

"What if someday something bad happens to us? Maybe someone will extend a hand to us."

For some, the migrants' gratitude is reason enough to give. A migrant boarding the train is stunned when, without a word, a man emerging from his house puts a large sandwich stuffed with scrambled eggs into his hands. The migrant, his voice cracking with emotion, says, "We could never keep going forward without people like this. These people give you things. In Chiapas, they take things away."

Some migrants who haven't eaten in days sob when they are handed a bundle of food. Other times, thanks come in a small gesture: a smile, a firm handshake before they move on.

Some townspeople have decided that giving migrants food and prayers is not enough. They invite strangers to stay, giving them shelter, sometimes for months at a time. There is a great risk in housing migrants: one could be accused of immigrant smuggling.

In one town, for more than two decades, priests leading the local church fought for the rights of workers and the poor. The church members were distressed to see groups of migrants huddling to sleep along the nearby tracks in the freezing rain. They saw many migrants injured, some from trying to escape capture, others by the train. They invited migrants inside for shelter.

Police officers started to run into the church to arrest migrants hiding inside; sometimes the officers' guns were drawn. One day, church members watched several *migra* officers come in and arrest four migrants. The officers hauled migrants by the hair and twisted their wrists behind their backs before throwing them into the back of their pickups.

"Help us! They're going to hit us!" one migrant cried out from the police pickup truck.

"Shut up!" one of the officers said, hitting the migrant with a nightstick several times.

Afterward, the incensed priest, a crowd of a hundred around him, demanded that the police let the migrants go. "This is a church. You have violated this place. Release them!" the priest said.

He organized teams that would rush out on a moment's notice to aid a migrant being abused by the police.

Sometimes whole communities stand up to the police.

Residents of El Campesino el Mirador, a railside hamlet nestled at the foot of a mountain, tell this story:

El Campesino el Mirador was policed by officers from nearby Nogales. One afternoon in late May 2000, a northbound freight train pulled onto a siding to let a southbound train pass. At that moment, police officers emerged from a bar by the tracks. Townspeople say the officers looked drunk. The police saw about fifty migrants on top of the stopped train and headed toward the freight cars to arrest them. Migrants jumped off and ran toward the mountain.

The police gave chase. Townspeople say the officers began to shoot. One bullet hit a Honduran girl, seventeen or eighteen years old, in the arm. She was eight months pregnant and said it was because she had been raped by a policeman in Chiapas.

The girl clawed her way up the mountain. After about one hundred yards, she reached a small concrete platform. On the platform stood a white cross. Panting and bleeding, she stopped, unable to go farther.

Three police officers caught up to her, grabbed her hair, kicked her, and beat her with their nightsticks.

"Leave me alone!" she cried. "You've already shot me. I'll lose this child."

María Enriqueta Reyes Márquez, thirty-eight, climbed up to the cross. She says she could see that a bullet had splintered a bone in the girl's arm. "It's as if they were hitting a dog," she recalls, her eyes brimming with tears. "They treat dogs better than that. They don't punish criminals, but they beat up these poor folks. Why? Why?"

Reyes says she demanded: "Stop hitting her." She and about fifty other people encircled the girl and the cross. They turned on the officers. "Cowards!" "Why are you hitting her?"

Two of the officers ran down the hillside, away from the angry mob. Someone kicked the third in the buttocks until he ran as well.

To protect migrants from corrupt police, individuals have also invited migrants to sleep in their own homes. María del Carmen Ortega García, a barrel-chested woman with a big smile, lets migrants sleep in a room in her house in Veracruz. Ortega started small, offering migrants a cup of coffee, then a place to bathe. They remind her of her eighteen-year-old son. In 1995 he was deported from California. She does not know what happened after he was driven across the border. She never heard from him again.

Others simply hide migrants from the police. Another townsperson in Veracruz, Baltasar Bréniz Ávila, empathizes with migrants. His two sons walked for days to enter the United States, through searing heat and with little drinking water. They dodged snakes, as well as bandits trying to assault them. Now they work as car washers in Orange County, California. "When I help someone here, I feel like I'm giving food to my children," Bréniz says. "I bet people help them, too."

Bréniz, who lives two blocks from the train tracks, had fed a twenty-five-year-old Honduran migrant some tacos. The man was on his porch, getting ready to leave, when a blue-and-white state police car cruised down the dirt road.

Bréniz whisked the migrant inside. The police knocked. "Turn him over! He's a migrant. We're going to arrest him. If you don't turn him over, we'll arrest you, too, for being a smuggler."

The police had pistols and machine guns. Bréniz knew that people charged with smuggling can spend years in jail. Bréniz, who sells rustic chairs door to door, tried to mask the terror he felt inside. He politely said there was no reason to turn the man over. He told them the visitor was a relative from an outlying farm. The police retreated.

Bréniz let the migrant stay for an hour, until he was sure the coast was clear.

NEW CARGO

As the train nears the town of Córdoba, the migrants finish their water, knowing it is tricky to jump off the train and run fast with a bottle in their hands. Enrique grabs the bag of rolls he got from the food throwers. He is hungry, but he saves the rolls for later; he fears they will be all he has to eat for a while. As the train slows, he leaps and runs.

He avoids the station's security guards and eases to a walk. He sits on a sidewalk one block north of the station. Two police officers approach.

His odds are better if he does not bolt. Fleeing would look suspicious. He tucks his bag of rolls into a crevice. He swallows his fright and tries to look unconcerned.

The officers, in navy blue uniforms, walk straight up to him.

He does not move or even flinch. Cops can sense fear. They can tell if someone is illegal. You have to be calm, he says to himself. You can't seem afraid. Look them in the eye. Be brave.

Unlike the townspeople, the police do not bear gifts. They pull out pistols. "If you run, I'll shoot you," one says, aiming at Enrique's chest. They take him and two younger boys, sitting nearby, to a big shed by the railroad, where officers are holding twenty migrants. It is a full-scale sweep.

They line up the migrants against a wall. "Take everything out of your pockets."

Bribing the police is the only way for Enrique to keep himself from being deported back to Central America. He has thirty pesos, about three dollars, that he earned lifting rocks and sweeping near the tracks a few towns back. Some officers will let you go for twenty pesos. Others demand fifty—or more—and then turn you over to *la migra* to be deported anyway. Now he prays the coins he has will be enough.

One officer pats him down and says to empty his pockets.

Enrique drops his belt, a Raiders cap, and the thirty pesos. He glances at his fellow migrants. Each is standing behind a little pile of belongings.

"Get out! Leave!"

He will not be deported after all. But he pauses. He gathers up his courage. "Can I get my things back, my money?"

"What money?" the officer hisses. "Forget about it, unless you want to have your trip stop here."

Enrique turns his back and walks away.

Even in Veracruz, where strangers can be so kind, the authorities cannot be trusted.

Exhausted, Enrique retrieves his bag of rolls, climbs onto a flatbed truck, and sleeps. At dawn, he hears a train. He trots alongside a freight car and clambers aboard once more, still holding his rolls.

THE MOUNTAINS

As Enrique pushes north toward the United States, Mexico changes.

The tracks, smoother now, begin to climb. The air grows cooler. The train passes sixty-foot-tall stalks of bamboo. It crosses a long bridge over a deep canyon. It rolls through putrid white smoke that billows from a Kimberly-Clark factory that turns sugarcane pulp into tissues and toilet paper.

Back in Oaxaca, he rolled through cattle country. It was so hot, the tracks behind him looked like a squiggly line, warped by heat. In the humidity, green moss balls grew on the electrical wires by the tracks. He was drenched in sweat.

In Veracruz, he rode through rows of silvery pineapple plants and lush fields of tall, thin sugarcane stalks that brushed up against the train. He saw homes where people put day-old tortillas on their tin roofs to dry. All around him were swamps and mosquitoes. He had to watch out for bees. He had heard that when smoke from the locomotive angers bees, they swarm and attack migrants on top of the cars.

The closer they get to the north, the more valuable the cargo carried on the train is—Volkswagens, Fords, and Chryslers. The trains are longer, better maintained, and they glide more smoothly. There are fewer riders on board now. Many migrants do not make it this far. On some trains, Enrique sees only a dozen others.

In Orizaba, the train pauses to change crews. Enrique asks a man standing near the tracks, "Can you give me one peso to buy some food?" The man inquires about his scars. They are from the beating he got on top of the train, a little more than a week ago now. The man gives Enrique fifteen pesos, about $1.50.

Enrique runs to buy soda and cheese to go with his rolls. He looks north. Beyond a range of verdant mountains he sees the snow-covered Pico de Orizaba, the highest summit in Mexico. Now the weather will turn icy cold, especially at night, much different from the steamy lowlands. Enrique begs two sweaters. Before the train pulls out, he runs from car to car, looking into the hollows at the ends of the hoppers, where riders occasionally discard clothing. In one, he finds a blanket.

As the train starts, Enrique shares the cheese, soda, and rolls he has saved with two boys he has met. The two boys are also headed for the United States. One is thirteen, the other is seventeen.

Enrique relishes his new friends. He loves how riders take care of one another, pass along what they know, and divide what they have. Migrants will often designate one person to look out for trouble while the others rest. They give one another advice. In places where migrants spring out from the shadows, sprinting to get on the moving train, migrants atop the cars shout out if the train is going dangerously fast.

"Don't do it! You'll get nailed!" they yell.

When Enrique lands an extra shirt or a tip about where to avoid the police, he shares. Other migrants have been generous with him. They have told him Mexican slang words they have learned. One offered a bit of soap when Enrique slipped into a shallow green river to bathe.

Enrique realizes that the friendships will be fleeting. Very few who set out together, including brothers, stay together until the end. Often migrants abandon an injured member of their group rather than risk being caught by the authorities.

As Enrique waits in Veracruz for a train to leave, a thirty-one-year-old Salvadoran tells how he recently watched a man get his right leg cut off as he was trying to elude *la migra* at a train stop. The Salvadoran stripped off his shirt and cinched it tightly around the man's leg to try and stop the bleeding. Then he ran away, fearful *la migra* would arrest him.

"Don't leave me!" the injured man cried out. The man died later that day.

Often, between train rides, Enrique prefers to sleep alone in a tall clump of grass, away from other migrants, knowing it will make him less of a target. Still, camaraderie often means survival. I could get to the north faster alone, Enrique figures, but I might not make it.

The mountains close in. Enrique invites his two friends to share the blanket he found earlier. Together they will be warmer. The three jam themselves between a grate and an opening on top of a hopper. Enrique stuffs rags under his head for a pillow. The car sways, and its wheels click-clack quietly. They sleep.

Now the train passes through the first of thirty-two tunnels. Sometimes the tail of the train hasn't left one tunnel before the locomotive dives into another. Outside is bright sun. Inside is darkness so black that riders cannot see their own hands. They shout, *"¡Ay! ¡Ay! ¡Ay! ¡Ay! ¡Ay!"* and listen to the deep, haunting echo. Enrique and his friends sleep on. Back in the daylight, the train rounds a hillside. The freight cars creak as they turn the curves. Below, a valley is filled with fields of corn, radishes, and lettuce, each a different hue of green.

El Mexicano is the longest tunnel. For eight minutes, the train vanishes inside. Black diesel smoke rises; it burns the lungs and stings the eyes. Some of the migrants bolt down the ladders in the dark, trying to escape the toxic haze. Enrique's eyes are closed, but his face and arms turn gray. His nose runs black soot. If a locomotive overheats inside the tunnel, the train must stop. Riders spring for the exits, gasping for clean air.

Ice forms on the train cars. Migrants huddle between the cars, seeking protection from the biting wind. Some are wearing just T-shirts. Their lips crack, their eyes grow dull. They pull their shirts over their mouths to warm themselves with their breath. When the train slows, they jog alongside to ward off the cold.

Some risk moving forward to the last of the train's three locomotives to press against the engine. Some stand in the warm wisps of diesel smoke. As night falls, some of the older migrants drink whiskey. Too much, and they tumble off. Others gather old clothing and trash and build fires on the ledges over the wheels of the hoppers. They hold their hands close to the fire, then press their palms to their frigid faces.

At the first light, the tracks straighten and level out. At one and a half miles above sea level, the train accelerates to thirty-five miles per hour. Enrique awakens. He sees cultivated cactus on both sides. Directly in front rise two huge pyramids—the pre-Aztec metropolis of Teotihuacán.

Then he sees housing developments. A billboard for Paradise Spa. A sewage ditch. Taxis. The train slows for the station at Lechería. Enrique gets ready to run.

He is in Mexico City.

SUSPICION

Enrique starts knocking on doors, begging for food. But the Veracruz hospitality has vanished. In Mexico City, people are edgy and often hostile, especially toward migrants.

"I'm afraid of them," one woman near the tracks says, wrinkling her nose. "They talk funny. They're dirty."

Another woman, who is soft-spoken and wears silver-rimmed spectacles and a gold cross on a chain around her neck, turns cold when she is asked about migrants. She tells a story about a young man who was attacked, robbed, and raped by a group of male migrants, and left naked and nearly dead.

Before, she had felt pity for migrants, she says. "After that, people closed their doors." She wonders how many among the innocent migrants traveling north are dangerous men, running from the law in their own countries. Now when migrants ask her, several times a day, for help—a taco, a coffee, a shirt, or a pair of socks—she always turns them down flat.

The city is dangerous enough as it is, she adds. In Mexico

City, crime is rampant. Churches hire armed guards to ensure peaceful services.

Enrique notices that Mexicans are quick to defend their right to migrate to the United States. "Jesus was an immigrant," he hears them say. But most won't give Central Americans who have arrived in their country food, money, or jobs.

Enrique goes house to house, hoping for mercy. Finally, at one house, he receives another gift: a woman offers him tortillas, beans, and lemonade.

Now he must hide from the state police, who guard the depot at Lechería, a gritty industrial neighborhood on the northwestern outskirts of Mexico City. Gray smog hovers over the smokestacks. There is a scrap metal recycling plant, a sprawling Goodyear tire factory, and a plastics factory.

Lechería is thirteen miles from the heart of Mexico's rail system. Still, the station here bustles with activity. The railroad tracks are littered with broken dolls, old tires, dead dogs, and worn shoes. Enrique must avoid *la migra*—the authorities sometimes show up at the station in unmarked cars. Most migrants at the station hide between or inside boxcars or in the grass.

Enrique crawls into a three-foot-wide concrete gutter pipe, one of several strewn in a field north of the station. The field is filled with cows and sheep and bursting with yellow and purple flowers.

Outside the gutter pipe where Enrique hides, trains clang and crash as workers add and subtract cars, forming trains that are nearly a mile long.

Enrique must pick trains wisely. He knows some train companies use fewer security guards than others. He looks out for those. Enrique chooses a ten-thirty p.m. northbound train. It travels all the way to the Texas border, mostly at night, when the dark will make it harder to spot him. Enrique and his two new friends from the train pick a boxcar. The boys load cardboard to lie on in order to stay clean.

Enrique spots a blanket on a nearby hopper. He climbs a ladder to get it, and hears a loud buzz from overhead. Live wires carry electricity above the trains for 143 miles north. Signs warn DANGER—HIGH VOLTAGE. But many of the migrants cannot read. And they don't even need to touch the wires to be killed; the electricity arcs outward up to twenty inches.

Enrique climbs the hopper car. Carefully, he snatches a corner of the blanket and yanks it down. Then he scrambles back to his boxcar and settles into a bed that he and his friends have fashioned out of straw they found inside.

Soon, he tells himself, he might make it to the border. It is within his grasp.

The landscape turns more and more desolate—sand and brush, jackrabbits and snakes. They cross boulders, dry riverbeds, and canyons with sheer rock walls. They plow through a heavy fog, and Enrique sleeps.

The boys jump off the train early, half a mile south of San Luis Potosí, where sixty-four railroad security officers guard the station. Enrique goes in search of food. One person gives him an orange. Another gives him three tacos. He shares them with his friends.

Until now, Enrique has opted to keep moving, finding food and money as quickly as possible before moving on. Once, in Chiapas, he survived on mangoes for three days. But here the countryside is too desolate and dry for a migrant to live off the land. Begging is always risky. There are no fruit trees or fields in sight, just factories that make glass and furniture. He needs to work if he is going to survive. Besides, he does not want to reach America penniless. He has heard that U.S. ranchers shoot migrants who come to beg.

He trudges up a hill to the small home of a brick maker. Politely, Enrique asks the man for food. The brick maker offers yet another kindness: if Enrique will work at the brickyard, he will get both food and a place to sleep. Happily, Enrique accepts.

Some Central American migrants say Mexican employers exploit them. The employers refuse to pay for work the migrants have done, or pay only a fraction of the minimum wage. But the brick maker does better than that: he pays Enrique well and gives the boy shoes and clothing.

For a day and a half, Enrique works at the brickyard, shoveling clay. At the end of the day, covered in clay and manure dust, he bathes in a cattle trough. At night, he sleeps in a shed on a dirt floor he shares with one of his friends from the train.

It is the first time on his journey that he has stopped running. He has grown used to living for the moment. Now, for the first time, he pauses to reflect. He thinks about hugging his mother when they are together again.

"I have to get to the border," Enrique tells his friend.

He wonders: Should he risk taking another train? In all of his attempts, he has survived more than thirty train rides. This time, freight cars have brought him 990 miles from Tapachula, near Guatemala. Is he pushing his luck to keep traveling this way?

The brick maker offers Enrique advice. Take a shuttle van through the checkpoint north of town, he tells him, then a bus to another town called Matehuala. Finally, hitchhike on a truck from there to Nuevo Laredo. There, only a river, the Rio Grande, will separate you from Texas. Enrique thanks the brick maker for his advice and collects his pay, 120 pesos. He buys a toothbrush and an 83-peso bus ticket. Three hours later, a pink archway welcomes him to Matehuala.

There, he walks to a truck stop. Matehuala is on a principal route for truckers headed to the United States. Fleets of eighteen-wheelers roll by.

"I don't have any money," he tells every driver he sees. "Can you give me a ride however far north you are going?"

One after another, they turn him down. Many, having made the lonely haul from Mexico City, would love to have the company for the remaining 380 miles to the border. Still, if they said yes, police might accuse them of smuggling to justify asking for bribes. Moreover, some of the truckers fear that migrants might assault them.

Finally, at ten a.m., one driver takes the risk. Enrique pulls himself up into the cab of a truck hauling beer.

"Where are you from?" the driver asks.

Honduras.

"Where are you going?" The driver has seen boys like Enrique before. "Do you have a mom or dad in the United States?"

Enrique tells him about his mother.

A sign at Los Pocitos says: CHECKPOINT IN 100 METERS. The truck idles in line. Then it inches forward. The driver is ready. You are my assistant, he declares to Enrique. I am your assistant, Enrique repeats back.

Federal police called *judiciales* ask the driver what he is carrying. They want his papers. They peer at Enrique.

But the officers do not ask any questions.

A few feet farther on, soldiers stop each vehicle to search for drugs and guns. Two young recruits wave them through. Enrique exhales a sigh of relief.

The scenery changes again. Joshua trees give way to low-lying scrub brush. The driver clears two more checkpoints. As he nears the Rio Grande, he stops to eat. He buys Enrique a plate of eggs and refried beans and a soda, another gift.

Sixteen miles before the border, he sees a sign: REDUCE YOUR SPEED. NUEVO LAREDO CUSTOMS.

Don't worry, the driver says, *la migra* check only the buses.

The next sign says: BIENVENIDOS A NUEVO LAREDO. Welcome to Nuevo Laredo.

The driver drops him off outside the city, near its airport, just past the Motel California. With the thirty pesos he has left, Enrique takes a bus that winds into the Plaza Hidalgo, a city park the size of a square block, in the heart of Nuevo Laredo.

Nuevo Laredo is a border town alongside the Río Bravo, as

the river is known here. Called the Rio Grande in the United States, the river divides Mexico from Texas.

Enrique marvels at how far he has come, how close he has come to getting caught and deported over and over again. Time after time, his luck has held. His heart swells with enormous hope. This hope is fragile. It could be punctured like a balloon in an instant. The thought of doing a *ninth* trip after he has come this far is nauseating. He must remain cautious.

Enrique has no money. He pivots his head to look around the Plaza Hidalgo. It is full of people. Some are migrants, who sit on the steps of the big clock tower. Others are smugglers, who circulate, offering, in a whisper, to take people over to the United States for a good price. Where does he go from here? Whom can he trust to ask for advice?

Through sheer chance, he spots a Honduran man whom he met on the train. Enrique races over to him. The man offers to help; he takes Enrique to an encampment along the Rio Grande. Enrique likes it. He decides to stay until he can cross.

That night, as the sun sets, Enrique stares across the Rio Grande and gazes at the United States. It looms as a mystery.

Somewhere over there lives his mother. She has become a mystery, too. He was so young when she left that he can barely remember what she looks like: curly hair, eyes like chocolate. Her voice is a distant sound on the phone.

Enrique has spent forty-seven days bent on nothing but surviving. Now, as he thinks about her, he is overwhelmed.

6

ON THE BORDER

"You are in American territory," a Border Patrol agent shouts through a bullhorn. "Turn back."

Sometimes Enrique strips and wades into the Rio Grande to cool off and wash away the sweat and grime. But the bullhorn always stops him. He goes back.

"Thank you for returning to your country."

Enrique is stymied. For days, he has been stuck in Nuevo Laredo. He has been watching, listening, and trying to plan. Somewhere across this milky green ribbon of water is his mother.

Enrique embraces the campsite as his temporary new home. It is safer for him than anywhere else in Nuevo Laredo, a city of half a million residents. It is swarming with *la migra* and all kinds of police. The camp is at the bottom of

117

a narrow, winding path that slopes to the river. A clump of reeds hides it from the U.S. immigration authorities' constant surveillance.

Enrique shares a soiled, soggy mattress with three other migrants. Still others lie on pieces of cardboard. For their clothing, they use "the closet"—a wire spring standing upright, from a mattress stripped of everything but its coils. Each resident of the camp has a space on one of the bare coils on which to hang his shirt and pants.

The leader of the river camp is El Tiríndaro. He usually wants drugs or beer as payment for letting migrants stay in his camp. He is a kind of "coyote," or smuggler, known as a *patero*. He smuggles people into the United States by pushing them across the river on inner tubes while paddling like a *pato*, or duck.

In addition to smuggling, El Tiríndaro tattoos people and sells clothing migrants have left on the riverbank to make money for drugs. When the drugs take hold, El Tiríndaro hallucinates. Sometimes he is so slowed by heroin that he can barely stand up or move.

The campsite has become a home for migrants, smugglers, drug addicts, and criminals. Some are just passing through, staying only a few days. Others have been stuck there for months, waiting for the right time to sneak across the border. One migrant, a fellow Honduran, has lived on the river for seven months. He has been caught every time he tried entering the United States. He has descended into depression and a life of glue sniffing, he says. Enrique listens. The migrants here call Enrique "El Hongo," the Mushroom, because he is quiet, soaking everything in.

Enrique clings to the camp, where he is protected. Because he is so young, everyone at the camp looks after him. When he leaves during the day, someone walks him through the brush to the road and always yells, "Be careful!" They warn him against heroin. They offer tips on which parts of the city are thick with police, places he should avoid.

Each week, El Tiríndaro gives police officers who patrol the river a 10 percent cut of his earnings as a smuggler. Because of these bribes, the police show leniency toward anyone at the camp. Nonetheless, police still regularly show up at the river and check migrants' pockets for drugs, and they help themselves to whatever change is there. They pick on the migrants because they figure they can get away with it.

Sometimes Enrique is too afraid to venture into Nuevo Laredo to drink from a faucet in a park. He takes water from the river, which carries raw sewage from dozens of towns. People tell him of a superstition: Drink from the Río Bravo, and you'll be stuck in Nuevo Laredo forever. He risks it anyway. The water tastes heavy, but it does not make him sick.

The camp is a hard place for Enrique to sleep in. It is noisy all night with the sounds of migrants coming and going as they try to cross the river. U.S. Border Patrol bullhorns bark, warning them back. Enrique can hear cars at a U.S. entry checkpoint a few blocks away.

All around is the smell of excrement from goats and from the campers, whose bathroom is the surrounding grass. The camp is strewn with trash. Red ants cover the ground, and millions of gnats hover over the river. In the daytime, it is scorching hot.

At night, Enrique gazes across the Rio Grande at the United States. Before him, on the American side of the border, he can see a church steeple, train tracks, and three antennas with blinking red lights.

It is almost May 2000, nearly two months since Enrique left home the last time. Enrique has spent forty-seven days bent on nothing but surviving. This is his eighth attempt to reach the north; he has pushed forward 1,800 miles. By now his mother must have called Honduras again. The family must have told her that he was gone. His mother must be worrying. He has to telephone her to let her know he is coming soon.

The last time he spoke to her, she was in North Carolina. He has no idea if she is still there, or where that is, or how to reach it. He used telephones so rarely in Honduras that he didn't even think to memorize his mother's number in case his scrap of paper was taken from him or lost.

Happily, he remembers one number back home—at a tire store where he worked. He will call and ask his old employer to find his aunt Rosa Amalia or his uncle Carlos and get his mother's number. Then Enrique will call back and get the number from his old boss. To make the two calls, he will require two telephone cards at fifty pesos apiece. When he phones his mother, he'll call collect.

He cannot beg a hundred pesos. He will have to get work.

For migrant children and teens, there are few options: shining shoes, selling gum or candy on the sidewalk, or washing cars. He'll wash cars.

Each evening, without fail, Enrique goes to the Nuevo Laredo city hall with a large plastic paint bucket and two rags. It takes courage to go; he knows he could get caught. From a spigot on the side of the building, he fills a bucket. He goes to parking spots across the street from a bustling taco stand.

Unlike workers at other businesses, those at the taco stand do not run him off. One of his rags is red. Each time someone arrives to eat dinner, he waves the red rag to guide the customer into a parking space, like a ground crew member ushering a jetliner to its arrival gate.

Usually there is competition. Two or three other migrants set up their buckets along the same sidewalk.

A woman in a blue dress pulls in to a parking space in a white Pontiac Bonneville.

"May I wash your windows?" Enrique asks. She nods and walks toward the taco stand. Enrique wipes the front of the car, then the side windows, moving his hand, with its fingers splayed across a rag, in quick, ever-growing circles. He walks around the car, wiping and wiping. He cleans inside, even the floorboards. The moon is out, but it is ninety degrees. Sweat trickles down his face. He must finish before the woman's tacos are ready.

She returns, fumbles for her car keys, gets in, then puts two coins—three and a half pesos—in his hand. *"Gracias,"* he says.

Most drivers turn down his services. He sighs. In eight

hours, scrambling after every car that pulls in, he makes only twenty pesos, about two dollars.

The air around the taco stand fills with the aroma of barbecue. Enrique watches workers pull strips of meat from a vat, put them on large chopping blocks, and cut them up. Customers sit at long stainless steel tables and eat. Sometimes, when the stand closes, the servers slip him a couple of tacos.

A LIFELINE

Otherwise, for his only meal every day, Enrique depends upon the Parroquia de San José, or St. Joseph's Parish. The parish church gives food cards to migrants. The cards are like gold. Sometimes they are stolen and sold for money. Migrants who bathe in the river leave their cards on the bank and carry rocks into the water to throw at anyone who tries to take them. With the card from this and a second church, Enrique can count on one meal a day for fifteen days.

The priest at the Parroquia de San José is Father Leonardo López Guajardo, known as Padre Leo. In Nuevo Laredo, Padre Leo is not a typical priest. Other priests in town wear nice watches and rings and act important. Padre Leo is so disheveled that visitors sometimes mistake him for one of the poor, dirty migrants sitting outside. He wears the same pants for days, stained and dirty from hauling boxes of ripe vegetables, food for the migrants. His favorite pair has frayed cuffs and a small tear in the rear.

During Mass, Padre Leo doesn't read from the Bible much.

He conveys his message through jokes or by spinning a lesson out of a popular movie or song. He does not stand at the altar; he paces up and down the church aisle's pink floor in his white robe, which he wears with broken-down sneakers. As he paces, he mops copious quantities of sweat from his balding head with a large white towel. A microphone in his left hand, the towel in his right, he preaches.

He is humble and lives modestly. He gives his salary to the church to help it pay staff salaries. When someone gave him a nice truck, he sold it to pay church utility bills. His car, which he rarely drives, to save gas and help the environment, is a tiny Mazda purchased for four hundred dollars. The driver's door won't open from the outside, the vinyl dash is shredded, and the front seat has a huge hole in it. He prefers to pick up donations of bread and clothing on his rickety blue bicycle.

"Either we are with the poor, or we are not. God teaches us to help the poor. Any other interpretation is unacceptable," he says. To Padre Leo, the people most in need in Nuevo Laredo are migrants. They go for days without food, for months without resting their heads on a pillow; they are defenseless against an onslaught of abuses. His vow is to restore a bit of their dignity.

"He saw that these people are the most vulnerable, the most disliked by the local population. So he gave himself to them," says a church volunteer.

Padre Leo gave up the two-bedroom priest's apartment attached to the church so that female migrants would have a safe place to sleep. He settled himself into a tiny room off the pantry.

A steady stream of migrants flows into the church. Padre Leo attends to them one by one. He takes down each individual's information, then gives him or her a meal card. He helps arrange to pick up money wired by relatives in the United States.

To help the migrants look more presentable, he gives away most of the few shoes and clothes he owns. He brings a hair-cutter to the church. A doctor treats the migrants' illnesses for free. If they need blood, Padre Leo is the first to donate.

Some parishioners thought the priest was crazy to attract what they saw as bums and delinquents to their neighborhood. They objected to helping migrants at all. "This was a good neighborhood—until you brought *your* people," they complained. What if some of them were dangerous criminals fleeing prosecution in their own countries? Meanwhile, their church, one of the poorest in the city, was falling apart. The pews were decrepit and the padre hadn't installed air-conditioning, despite summer temperatures that reach 120 degrees. A church survey showed that many parishioners didn't attend church because of the migrants.

Once, the local director of *la migra* threatened to lock up the priest for several years on smuggling charges if he didn't bar migrants from entering his church. Padre Leo promised to behave—and then ignored the warning.

Now three-quarters of the people in his parish agree with his work. "We should say thanks that we don't have to go through this—but maybe with a bit of bread, a smile, you can lessen their load," a volunteer says. Without the church's help, she adds, the migrants would be even more desperate, and the impact on the city would be worse.

The volunteer, who cooks dinner for migrants daily, says, "Padre Leo has taught me to give to others without expecting anything in return."

Each night, like clockwork, Leti Limón, a volunteer, swings open the church's yellow double doors.

"Who's new?" she calls out.

"Me! Me!" migrants—men and boys—cry out from the courtyard. They all rush to the door, jostling one another to get in.

"Get in line! Get in line!" Limón shouts. She is poor herself; she cleans houses across the river in Texas, for twenty dollars apiece. But she has helped to feed these migrants for a year and a half, figuring that Jesus would approve. She issues the newcomers beige cards and punches the cards of those who enter. A parish priest counts 6 percent children.

One by one, the migrants stand behind chairs at a long table. At the head is a mural of Jesus, his hands extended toward the plates of tacos, tomatoes, and beans. Above Jesus are his words: COME TO ME, ALL YOU WHO ARE WEARY AND FIND LIFE BURDENSOME.

The lights dim, and two big fans spin to a stop so everyone can hear grace. In the still air, the room turns hot, nearly suffocating; perspiration trickles down the migrants' faces and soaks their shirts. A volunteer or one of the migrants begins the short prayer. Some who have not eaten in days grab at bread before they have finished saying grace.

A volunteer asks everyone to remove their hats, to please eat everything on their trays or give it to someone near them.

Chairs screech as everyone pulls them out at once. Spoons of stew touch lips before bottoms hit the seats. There are more migrants than chairs. Some eat standing. Others squat on the floor, plates balanced on their knees. They eat in quiet desperation. In a clatter of forks against plates, beans, stew, tomatoes, rice, and doughnuts disappear.

Afterward, opposite a portrait of the Virgin of Guadalupe, about a dozen of the migrants always gather around a map of Texas. It is covered in plastic, but fingerprints have blackened parts of it anyway. They discuss the state of the river. Is it high? Low? They tell how they will get to Texas crossing the Rio Grande.

COMPANIONSHIP

At church dinners Enrique meets other teenagers who hope to reach their mothers in the United States.

A sixteen-year-old boy, Ermis Galeano, is stuck, too. He and Enrique compare stories. Both are from Honduras. Both have been robbed. As with Enrique, bandits on top of a train struck Ermis in the face with a board. It tore out his front teeth, leaving two black holes. As with Enrique, the bandits left Ermis in his underwear, sobbing and bloody. They ripped up his scrap of paper with his mother's phone number on it, too, and tossed it to the wind. This is Ermis's third attempt to reach his mother.

Ermis's mother left when he was ten. She sent money, five letters, and fifteen photos. She called as often as she could afford to. It was not enough. He wanted to be with her. "My mom told me she loves me. No one else ever told me that," Ermis says.

Enrique and Ermis make another friend, a fifteen-year-old girl, Mery Gabriela Posas Izaguirre, or Gabi, as she prefers to be called. She tells them her story. Her mother, who was divorced, struggled to keep Gabi and her two brothers fed. Her mother sold most of what she had—tables, beds, pots and pans—to send the children to school. Finally, one afternoon in July 1999, Gabi came home from school to find only a note: "I'm going for a little while. I'm going to work very hard." Her mother left Gabi's older brother in charge and asked the children to pray three times a day: before they ate, slept, or went outside.

Gabi and her brothers ached for her. They began sleeping in her bed to feel near to her. Gabi would drift off smelling her mother's scent on the pillow. She missed feeling cared for. She dreamed that her mother was at home, scolding her in the morning, telling her to get to school on time. She imagined that they were going to the park. She missed teasing her for playing "old-fogy music"—Beethoven.

"The house felt sad, empty," Gabi says.

Every time the telephone rang, Gabi raced to answer it. "When are you coming home?" she begged her mother. Then she turned harsh: "Why did you bring us into the world, if you were going to leave us?" Of forty-eight children in her class, thirty-six had a parent in the United States, most often a mother.

At her new home in the northeastern United States, Gabi's mother cleaned houses and babysat two toddlers. One day she sent Gabi a Barbie doll. The toddlers had already torn open the box. Gabi seethed. She sat alone, envisioning her mother playing with these other children.

On the telephone, Gabi and her mother argued. "I'm taking care of other kids instead of you. Can you imagine what that's like?" her mother demanded. "You don't know what I've suffered."

Gabi didn't believe her. All she wanted was to be with her.

Winter came. Her mother called, crying. She was sick, lonely, and out of a job.

"I knew I had to go," Gabi said. "I thought: 'I'm young. I want to help her, so she can come home.'"

By Christmas of 1999, going to the United States had become an obsession.

Her mother was terrified that Gabi would make the trip alone. She could be raped. Gabi's twenty-six-year-old aunt, Lourdes Izaguirre, decided to take the journey with her. Together, they figured, they might be less vulnerable.

Gabi left behind her brothers. Gabi's aunt Lourdes walked away from her children, ages five and ten, and two younger siblings she was raising. She left all of them with her own mother. Back home, Aunt Lourdes was paid thirty dollars a week for making Tommy Hilfiger–labeled shirts. Even working full-time, she could not make enough to feed them all.

A smuggler promised to deliver Gabi and Aunt Lourdes for two thousand dollars up front, but he robbed and abandoned them in Tapachula, just inside the southern border of Mexico. They were deported to Guatemala. The two resolved to try again. This time, they would hike through the Lacandón jungle in the Mexican state of Chiapas. Gabi and Aunt Lourdes spent days washing people's clothes along the Usumacinta River in exchange for food. They asked every smuggler who went by if he would take them through the mountain pass. The smugglers demanded sex in exchange.

Angrily, Gabi refused.

Finally, four smugglers let them tag along with a group of eighty migrants who Gabi learned had paid between five and eight thousand dollars apiece. They put her up front to help cut a path in the jungle's dense vegetation. Gabi rebuffed constant demands for sex. She tried to look as ugly as possible. She hardly slept, never smiled or combed her hair. Her legs turned black with ticks. She felt as though bugs were eating her alive, but she dared not lift her skirt to remove them.

She kept repeating to herself: I have to get to my mother.

She and Aunt Lourdes switched to hitchhiking. But a *migra* agent caught them trying to walk around a checkpoint. The agent was a woman, Gabi says, who ordered them to strip and checked their clothing for hidden cash.

The agent scolded them for having so little money. If you can't pay me, why should I release you? she wanted to know.

"Please let us go," Gabi begged. "I'm going to help my mother."

"¡*Váyanse!* Go!" the agent said.

Finally, Gabi and Aunt Lourdes made it to Nuevo Laredo. Gabi tells Enrique she feels stuck here, too. Sometimes, she says, lowering her voice, she feels like she wants to die.

Aunt Lourdes begins to cry. "I feel bad for doing this. It wasn't worth it. I'd rather starve with my children. But I've come this far. I can't go back." She mortgaged her property and borrowed money from a neighbor for her journey. Her voice turns firm again. "I can't go back empty-handed." Gabi puts her arm around her aunt.

Outside the church after dinner, many migrants engage in a twisted kind of street therapy: Who has endured the worst, riding the trains? They measure trips not in days but in shoes lost, beatings taken, belongings robbed. They show off scars. "I walked four days." "I walked twenty-eight days!" They air feet covered in large blisters, toenails that have turned up from walking.

A young man sits on a green metal bench outside the church. He has been stuck here for weeks, and he trumps everyone. He slides up a leg of his black jeans and takes off a high-topped black sneaker, then a prosthesis. His right calf tapers into a pink stump.

HUNGRY FOR HOPE

The fifteen days on Enrique's meal cards pass quickly. He is still saving money for his two phone cards. Now he will have to spend money on food. He begins to eat as little as possible: crackers and soda. Sometimes, desperate to save money for the phone calls, Enrique does not eat at all.

Sometimes there is nothing left to do but to risk the cops, go downtown, and beg. He goes down to Avenida Guerrero with a friend. It is filled with tourists who spill across the border to shop, drink, dance, and hire prostitutes. Five-year-olds tap the tourists on the arm and ask them to buy packs of gum. Old women sit on sidewalks and extend their weathered hands, seeking a coin or two. Avenida Guerrero is thick with police. For a Central American without papers, it is treacherous ground.

But he is desperate. His friend leans on his arm, drags a foot, and pretends to be lame. They approach every tourist they see. "Want me to show you where the train hit me?" the friend offers, innocently. Slowly, he lifts the cuff of his pants.

People recoil. "No, no. Here!" They give a peso and scurry away.

Enrique and his friend retreat to the river before the police can catch them, with only enough to buy more crackers.

Enrique feels weak. Occasionally, local fishermen give him a fish they have caught. Friends at the camp share their meals of scrambled eggs or a bowl of soup.

The campmates share experiences before bed. They talk

about the poverty they came from; they would rather die than go back. They offer Enrique advice about crossing the river: Use an inner tube. Take a gallon of water. Find which spots are best to cross the river.

Enrique talks about María Isabel, and that she might be expecting. He hasn't spoken to her since his journey began and does not know for certain.

Enrique tells them about his mother. He says he is becoming extremely depressed. "I want to be with her," he says, "to know her." He stops.

"If you talk, it's better," a friend says gently.

But it gets worse. There is nothing to do but work and save money until he can call her. Then he will figure out how to cross the river to his mother. He doesn't know how long any of this will take.

Enrique feels anxious about staying too long in Nuevo Laredo. He fears being attacked by bandits. He hears of atrocities: knives, a rifle to the chest, beatings, demands for shoes and money.

Enrique sees gangsters hang out in front of the San José church. They act like dogs, sniffing out robbery prospects. Most of them are Salvadorans with MS tattooed on their foreheads and new black Nikes on their feet. "I'll pass you across the river. Give me two hundred pesos," they say to migrants walking by. Those who don't know any better follow the gangsters. They are taken to the riverbank and assaulted.

At the river camp, a Salvadoran gangster, covered in tattoos, threatens to thrash Enrique. A migrant MS from his old neighborhood in Honduras intervenes and spares Enrique a beating.

Enrique trembles with relief, fear, and rage as he hurries away from the gangsters.

El Tiríndaro never threatens Enrique; instead he is generous. He knows the sooner Enrique can save money to buy a phone card and call his mother, the sooner Enrique will pay for his smuggling services.

El Tiríndaro knows that Enrique cannot swim, so he paddles him back and forth on the water in an inner tube to quiet his fears. When the river level drops, it exposes the lower branches of willows lining the banks. They are draped with clothing that the migrants discard as they begin to wade out. Plastic bags, shorts, and underwear hang from the boughs like tattered Christmas ornaments. El Tiríndaro takes Enrique on the inner tube along the bank as he collects the clothing. They wash the clothes in the river, then sell them near the taco stand. El Tiríndaro lets Enrique keep a T-shirt they find.

One night, as Enrique walks the twenty blocks back to the river from washing cars, it rains. El Tiríndaro doesn't usually sleep at the camp when it rains. The camp, Enrique fears, will be too dangerous without El Tiríndaro there. He ducks into an abandoned house. It has gaping holes in the roof. He finds some cardboard and places it on a dry spot. He removes his sneakers and puts them and his bucket near his head. He has no socks, blanket, or pillow. He pulls his shirt up around his ears and breathes into it to stay warm. Then he lies down, curls up, and tucks his hands across his chest.

Lightning flashes. Thunder rumbles. Wind wails around the corners of the house. The rain falls steadily. On the highway, trucks hiss their brakes, stopping at the border before entering the United States. Across the river, the Border Patrol shines lights on the water, looking for migrants trying to cross.

With his bare feet touching a cold wall, Enrique sleeps.

MOTHER'S DAY

It is May 14, 2000, a Sunday when many churches in Mexico celebrate Mother's Day. The Parroquia de San José is packed with a large Mother's Day party. The women of Nuevo Laredo laugh, shout, and whistle as their sons dance with pillows stuffed under their shirts to make them look pregnant.

Every time Enrique goes to the Parroquia de San José, it makes him think about his mother, especially today. The church makes him homesick for Grandmother María, too, and their weekly walks to Mass when he was a child.

Migrants who are separated from their families try to ignore the celebrations. Migrant women weep for being so far from their children. Beneath their sense of hope is sadness and guilt. Each mother shares the same fears.

Daily, one woman prays: Don't let me die on this trip. If I die, my children will live on the street.

Many of the women became single mothers because they were unwilling to endure the more difficult parts of their relationships with men: drunkenness, beatings, mistresses. Alone, supporting their children is very difficult. To feed their children, to avoid prostitution, they leave.

Though many mothers expect the separation to be short, typically it lasts six to eight years, says Analuisa Espinoza, a Los Angeles Unified School District social worker who specializes in immigrants. By then, they and their children are strangers. Some mothers, picking up children from smugglers, hug the wrong ones.

Each of these young women could be his mother of eleven years ago, Enrique thinks.

He wonders what his mother looks like now.

"It's okay for a mother to leave," Enrique tells a friend, "but just for two or four years, not longer." He recalls Lourdes's promises to return for Christmas and how she never did. He remembers how he longed to have his mother with him each time his grandmother scolded him.

One thing, though: Lourdes always told him she loved him. "I've felt alone all my life," he says. "I don't know what it will be like to see her. She will be happy. Me too. I want to tell her how much I love her. I will tell her I need her."

Enrique has finally saved fifty pesos. Eagerly, he buys a phone card. He gives it to one of El Tiríndaro's friends for safekeeping. That way, if the police or gangsters catch him, they cannot steal it.

"I just need one more," he says. "Then I can call her."

Across the Rio Grande, Lourdes is thinking about Enrique. She has, indeed, learned that he is gone. But in her phone calls home, she never finds out where he went. She remembers their last telephone conversation. "I'll be there soon," he said. "Before you know it, on your doorstep." Day after day, she waits for him to call. Night after night, she cannot sleep more than three hours. She watches TV: migrants drowning in the Rio Grande, dying in the desert, ranchers who shoot them. Is one of them her son?

She imagines the worst and becomes terrified that she might never see Enrique again. His disappearance stirs up her bad memories of her ex-boyfriend Santos's disappearance when Diana was four years old. She is utterly helpless. She asks God to watch over Enrique, guide him.

On the afternoon of the Mother's Day celebration, three municipal police officers visit the camp. Enrique does not try to run, but he is jittery. They ignore him. Instead they take away one of his friends.

Enrique has no money for food, not even for crackers. He takes a hit of glue. It makes him sleepy, takes him to another world, eases his hunger, and helps him forget about his family. He lies on the mattress and talks to the trees. He cries. He talks about his mother. "I want to be near my mom. I want to be near her," he says over and over again until the fog in his mind lifts.

A friend catches six tiny catfish. He builds a fire out of trash. It grows dark. He cuts the fish with the lid from an aluminum can.

Enrique hovers nearby. "You know, Hernán, I haven't eaten all day."

Hernán guts the fish.

Enrique stands silently, waiting.

A SETBACK

It is May 15. Enrique has had a good night washing cars: he made sixty pesos. At midnight, he rushes to buy his second phone card. He puts only thirty pesos on it, gambling that his second call will be short.

Enrique saves his other thirty pesos for food.

He and his friends celebrate. He wants a tattoo. "A memory of my journey," he says.

El Tiríndaro offers to do it for free. Enrique wants black ink, but all El Tiríndaro has is green. Enrique pushes out his chest and asks for two names, so close together they are almost one. For three hours, El Tiríndaro digs into Enrique's skin. In gothic script, the words emerge:

EnriqueLourdes.

His mom, he thinks happily, will scold him.

The next day just before noon, he stirs from his dirty mattress. He borrows some toothpaste, squats at the river, dips his toothbrush into the murky water, and cleans his broken teeth. They still ache from the beating he took on top of the train a few weeks ago. So does his head, which throbs constantly. A dark pink welt an inch long scars his left forehead. He still cannot see well with his left eye, and the lid sags. His arms and legs are purple with bruises, and he has been wearing the same clothes for days.

He is hungry. Hours pass. His hunger grows. Finally, he cannot stand it. He retrieves the first phone card from the friend who is holding it, and he sells it for food.

He uses all of the money to buy crackers, the cheapest thing that will fill his stomach.

Now he has gone from two phone cards to one, worth only thirty pesos. He regrets surrendering to his hunger. If only he can earn twenty pesos more. Then he will go ahead and phone his old boss and hope that his aunt or uncle will call back, so he won't need a second card.

But someone has stolen his bucket. Without it, he is lost: he used it for sitting when he waited for cars to clean near the taco stand, for chopping food, for washing his feet, and, above all, for earning a living.

When he thinks about giving up, he tries to reassure himself: I know my day will come. I know I shouldn't get desperate. After eating his crackers, he lies on his mattress, stone quiet, and looks at the sky. His friend can see that he is depressed. Since Enrique has been at the river, he has watched thirty other men and boys sleep at the camp, pay a smuggler, then cross the river into the United States.

The friend tries to cheer him up. He urges him not to despair.

Someone at camp sees Enrique's angst and lends him a bucket. Enrique trudges back out to the car wash across from the taco stand. He sits on the bucket. Carefully, he pulls up his T-shirt. There, in an arch just above his belly button, is his tattoo, painfully raw. *EnriqueLourdes*. Now the words mock him. He is deeply exhausted. For the first time, he is ready to go back home. But he holds back his tears and lowers his shirt. As homesick as he is for Honduras, he refuses to give up.

THE MOMENT

Friends at camp warn Enrique against crossing the Rio Grande by himself. It's a treacherous trek from the moment you step into the river. There are whirlpools below the water, ready to take you under, and Border Patrol helicopters skimming above the water, whipping up high waves that toss you around.

His campmates tell Enrique he needs a guide, someone who knows the route ahead.

And when you make it across the river into the United States, they warn, walking across Texas alone is out of the question. Without a guide, it is easy to get lost and wander in circles in the sameness of the brushlands. The trek to San Antonio takes seven or eight days, in desert heat of up to 120 degrees, with rattlesnakes, cactus needles that cut you, saucer-size tarantulas, and wild hogs with tusks. Some migrants, dehydrated and delirious, commit suicide.

Some are shot by Texas ranchers as they try to beg or steal food or drink. Ranchers have become increasingly riled by immigrants who trespass. Some ranchers sit on their front porches with pistols in their laps. Most immigrants are good, they say, but the bad ones pack drugs, break into your place, and steal things.

On the Texas side of the river, the Border Patrol agents are skilled and dogged. In 2000 alone, the year Enrique was trying to enter the United States, 108,973 migrants were caught near Laredo. As Enrique prepares to make his attempt, the Border Patrol has been on a hiring frenzy. In all, the government has hired more than 5,600 additional agents since 1993 to expand its forces along the southern U.S. border. Agents are equipped with helicopters, night-vision goggles, thermal imaging that picks up body heat, and sensors that detect footsteps along immigrant trails. They move the sensors constantly, so smugglers and migrants don't know where they are buried.

At supper at the San José church, Enrique meets men who have been deported by border agents. One man who snuck through the desert alone hasn't eaten in five days. When he arrives at the church, his brown shirt, torn to shreds by cactus, hangs in pieces on his body. His arms are cut up and bleeding, pricked with thistles and thorns. He is caked with mud. The bottoms of both feet are covered by huge yellow blisters and his toenails have turned black. He had to kill five rattlesnakes as he walked. He begs for a glass of water and a shower.

Everything Enrique hears makes him terrified of snakes and scorpions. In the Texas desert, snakes come out to hunt at night, when it is cooler. That is when migrants are on the move. They fumble forward in the dark, afraid to use a flashlight. Some rely, instead, on superstitions: Take a pregnant woman with you, and the snakes will sleep as you pass by. Put three peppercorns under your tongue for good luck. There are copperhead snakes, coral snakes, cottonmouth snakes, and the blue indigo snake, so long and fast it can kill a rattlesnake.

There is a bumper crop this year, and the drought has made them more aggressive.

Many times, when Enrique falls asleep, he has the same nightmare: A snake has bitten him in the mouth. He cannot call out for help.

El Hongo listens to his friends. He decides against going alone. Why should I die doing this? he asks himself.

Enrique knows he cannot trust just any smuggler. Back home in Honduras, most smugglers are honest; they must uphold their reputations if they want business. Here along the border, smugglers can rob, rape, or abandon their clients without any consequences. Many migrants at the church return with horror stories about smugglers.

Enrique has seen El Tiríndaro take a number of migrants across the river, always at night, usually one or two at a time, paddling furiously in their inner tubes.

El Tiríndaro does not work alone; he is part of a network with other smugglers. He has partners on the other side of the river, people who hide migrants if Border Patrol agents are in pursuit. A middle-aged man and a young woman, both Latinos, drive El Tiríndaro and his clients north, helping them maneuver around Border Patrol checkpoints in Texas. After the last checkpoint, El Tiríndaro returns to Nuevo Laredo, and the couple and others in the network deliver the clients to their destinations.

When El Tiríndaro takes migrants over, Enrique notices, they are never caught and sent back. El Tiríndaro has studied the movements of the Border Patrol so long, says Enrique's friend, that he knows what each agent does every eight hours, during the shift change.

But he charges $1,200.

Enrique makes a decision: When he can afford to call his mother, he will ask her to hire El Tiríndaro as a smuggler. I know, he says to himself, that he won't strand me.

❖ ❖ ❖

On May 18, Enrique awakens to find that someone has stolen his right shoe. Shoes are almost as important as food and his mother's telephone number. He can think of every pair that has helped him come north. On this trip alone, there were seven. Blue shoes, white shoes, leather work boots, Nike sneakers. He has bought, borrowed, or traded for them. All have fallen apart or been stolen. But never only one.

He spots a sneaker floating near the riverbank. He snags it. It is for a left foot. Now he has two left shoes. Bucket in hand, he hobbles back to the taco stand, begging along the way. People give him a peso or two. He washes a few cars, and it starts to rain. Astonishingly, he has put together twenty pesos in all.

Enrique feels joy and anxiety as he walks back to the camp in his two left shoes.

He now has enough for a phone card.

PADRE LEO'S HELP

It is May 19. There is only one way Enrique's plan will work. Padre Leo at the San José church lets migrants phone from the church if they have cards. Each day, he serves as their telephone assistant and alerts them if they have received a call. Enrique will have to trust the priest to find him if his aunt and uncle call back.

In late afternoon, Enrique reaches his old boss on the church telephone. He tells him to ask his aunt and uncle to call the San José church. Two hours later, Padre Leo bellows Enrique's name. As always, word spreads through the courtyard like wildfire: Someone named Enrique has a phone call.

"Are you all right?" asks Uncle Carlos.

"Yes, I'm okay," Enrique says hurriedly. "I want to call my mom. I've lost the phone number."

Uncle Carlos reads it, digit by digit, into the phone. Carefully, Enrique writes them down, one after another, ten digits on a shred of paper. Just as Uncle Carlos finishes, the phone dies. Uncle Carlos calls back. But Enrique is already out the church door. He cannot wait.

When he talks to his mom, he wants to be alone—he might cry. He runs to an out-of-the-way pay phone to call her. Collect.

He is nervous. Maybe she and her housemates have blocked the telephone to collect calls. Or what if she refuses to pay? First of all, it is expensive. Second of all, she told him, harshly, not to come north, but he disobeyed her. Each of the few times they talked, she urged him to study. This, after all, was why she left—to send money for school. But he has dropped out of school. Maybe she is angry at him. Maybe she doesn't even want to talk to him.

Heart in his throat, he heads to the small park not far from his camp.

It is seven p.m., a dangerous time for him to be away from the camp. Police patrol the park. If they saw him, he would be sure to catch their attention. He has two left shoes and jeans that are worn and torn; he looks too tattered to be in this neighborhood. He pulls the shred of paper from his pant pocket.

He lifts the receiver of a pay phone at the edge of the park.

Slowly, carefully, he unfolds his prize possession: her phone number. He listens in wonderment as his mother answers. She accepts the charges.

"*¿Mami?*"

At the other end, Lourdes's hands begin to tremble. Then her arms and knees. "*Hola, mi hijo.* Hello, my son. Where *are* you?"

"I'm in Nuevo Laredo. *¿Adónde estás?* Where are you?"

"I was so worried." Her voice breaks, but she forces herself not to cry. She wants to stay strong for him. She doesn't want him to break down, too. "North Carolina." She explains where that is.

Enrique's nerves ease.

"How are you coming? Get a coyote," she insists. She sounds worried. She says she knows of a good smuggler in Piedras Negras.

"No, no," he says. "I have someone here." Enrique trusts El Tiríndaro, but he costs $1,200.

She will get the money together, she promises. "Be careful," she says.

Despite the bond between them, the conversation is awkward. He and his mother are strangers.

But he can feel her love. He places the receiver in its cradle and sighs. At the other end, Lourdes finally cries.

Part III

Across the Border

7

DARK RIVER CROSSING

"If you get caught, I don't know you," says El Tiríndaro. He is stern.

It is one a.m. on May 21, 2000.

Enrique waits at the edge of the water. He nods. So do two other migrants, a Mexican brother and sister, waiting with him. They strip to their underwear. They will take their clothes in a plastic bag to keep them from getting wet.

Enrique tears up a small piece of paper and scatters it on the riverbank. It is his mother's phone number. He has memorized it. Now the agents cannot use it to locate and deport her.

Across the Rio Grande stands a fifty-foot pole equipped with U.S. Border Patrol cameras. In the darkness, Enrique cannot see any of the sport-utility vehicles that lurk on the other side of the river. But he knows they are there.

Enrique has seen smugglers ask migrants to grab hold of a long rope to cross the river. Others have the migrants lock arms and form a human chain. El Tiríndaro's strategy is more risky. He uses a black inner tube, which is bulky and easy for Border Patrol agents to spot. He can take only one or two people across at a time.

El Tiríndaro holds the inner tube. The Mexicans climb on. Enrique waits. El Tiríndaro takes the Mexican siblings to an island in the middle of the river.

El Tiríndaro returns, just as he promised. Enrique is relieved.

El Tiríndaro steadies the tube in the water. Carefully, Enrique climbs aboard. The river is swollen with rain. Two nights ago, it killed a youngster he knew. A whirlpool pulled him under. Up to three migrants in a single day have drowned along this stretch of river. Enrique cannot swim, and he is afraid.

El Tiríndaro places a plastic garbage bag on Enrique's lap. It contains dry clothing for the four of them. Then El Tiríndaro paddles and starts to push. A swift current grabs the tube and sweeps it into the river. Wind whips off Enrique's cap. Drizzle coats his face. He looks out for green snakes that skim along the cold waves. He holds on tight to the tube as it lurches, sloshes, and bounces.

All at once, Enrique sees a flash of white—one of the Border Patrol's SUVs, probably with a dog in back, inching along a trail above the river.

To his surprise, no bullhorn barks "Turn back." Just silence. Only the lapping of water against the tube.

Enrique and his paternal grandmother, María, who cared for him in Honduras.

Enrique's kindergarten graduation picture, shortly after his mother left.

Enrique, before he set off on his journey.

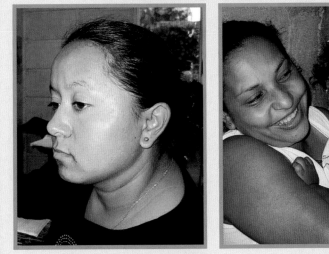

CLOCKWISE FROM TOP:

The heartfelt reunion of Enrique and his mother, Lourdes, in North Carolina.

Enrique's daughter, Jasmín, and her mother, María Isabel, in Tegucigalpa.

Enrique's sister, Belky, at the Tegucigalpa university where she studied.

Train jumpers from Honduras.

Train jumpers crossing a bridge near Tenosique, Tabasco, Mexico.

RETRANCA Nº 18   DESORTES D5

Train jumpers in Mexico headed northwest from Gregorio
Mendez, Tabasco, toward Palenque, Chiapas, Mexico.

An encampment next to the Rio Grande on the Nuevo Laredo side,
similar to the one Enrique found after he arrived in the Mexican city.

TOP: Enrique's son, Daniel, on the day he was born.

BOTTOM: Lourdes playing with two-month-old Daniel.

The inner tube wobbles on the waves. Enrique never re-
leases his grip. The dark sky is overcast, and the river is black.
In the distance, bits of light dance on the surface.

At last he sees the little island, overgrown with willows and
reeds. He seizes the limb of a willow. It tears off. With both
hands, he lays hold of a larger branch, and the inner tube
swings onto the mud and grass. They have crossed the southern channel, the first part of making it across this river. On the
other side of the island flows the northern channel. It is even
riskier because it is closer to the United States.

El Tiríndaro circles the tiny island on foot and looks across
the water. The white SUV reappears, moving slowly, less than
a hundred yards away. Its roof lights flash red and blue on the
water. Agents turn to aim a spotlight straight at the island.

Enrique and the Mexicans dive to the ground face-first.
He can think of nothing worse than being caught now. He is
closer to his mother than ever. Authorities would deport the
Mexicans back across the river, but they would send him all
the way back to Honduras.

Worse, he could sit in a Texas jail cell for months before the
United States processed the paperwork to deport him. There
is a juvenile prison in Liberty, Texas, forty-six miles northeast
of Houston, where many minors who are captured trying to
enter the United States alone and illegally are sent to await
deportation.

Immigrant children are brought to the jail shackled in
handcuffs. They are strip-searched and checked for money,
drugs, and weapons. Some as young as twelve are held in the

prison. They are housed, at times, in the same windowless cells as accused rapists and other felons. They are underfed and are barely allowed outside. They are given little information about when they might be brought before an immigration judge or deported. The guards know little, and most do not speak Spanish to explain to the children.

If Enrique was caught and sent to one of these jails, he could spend two or three months locked up before being sent back to Honduras. It would mean starting out for the ninth time. He swore to himself he would try for a year, no less, to get to the United States. In all, he has spent four months in his quest to reach his mother, but his strength and patience are breaking.

For half an hour on the river's island, everyone lies stone still. Crickets sing, and water rushes around the rocks. Finally, the agents seem to give up. El Tiríndaro makes certain, then returns to Enrique and the Mexicans.

Enrique whispers, "Take the others first." El Tiríndaro loads the two Mexicans onto the tube. Slowly, they lumber across the water.

Minutes later, El Tiríndaro returns. "Get over here," he says to Enrique. "Climb up." He has other instructions: Don't rustle the garbage bag holding the clothes, he whispers. Don't step on twigs. And don't paddle; it makes noise.

El Tiríndaro slips into the water behind the tube and kicks his legs beneath the surface. It takes only a minute or two. He and Enrique reach a spot where the river slows, and Enrique grabs a branch. They pull ashore and touch soft, slippery mud. In his underwear, Enrique stands for the first time on United States soil.

NEARLY FROZEN

As El Tiríndaro hides the inner tube, he spots the Border Patrol. He and the three migrants hurry along the edge of the Rio Grande until they reach a side stream of water called Zacate Creek.

"Get in," El Tiríndaro says.

Enrique walks into the frigid creek. He lowers himself until the water reaches his chin. His broken teeth chatter so hard it hurts; he cups a hand over his mouth, trying to stop them. For an hour and a half, they crouch in Zacate Creek in stone cold silence. A pipe connected to a sewage plant on the edge of Laredo, Texas, spills effluent into the water. Enrique can smell it.

At El Tiríndaro's command, Enrique and the others climb out of the water. Enrique, numb, falls to the ground, nearly frozen. "Dress quickly," El Tiríndaro says in an urgent whisper.

Enrique steps out of his wet underwear and tosses them away. They are his last possession from Honduras. He puts on his dry jeans and shirt, and his two left shoes—all things he has been given or found along the way.

Hidden in a thicket of bushes, El Tiríndaro offers everyone a piece of bread and a soda, but Enrique is too nervous to eat. This is the first time he can remember that food is something he does not want.

"This is the hard part," El Tiríndaro says. He starts to run. Enrique and the Mexicans race behind him. It is so dark it feels like they are running blind through a maze.

Finally, El Tiríndaro stops and glances nervously to the right and left. Nothing. "Follow me," he says.

Now he runs faster. Fear melts the icy numbness out of Enrique's legs. They sprint along narrow paths, into the dry upstream channel of Zacate Creek, under a pipe, then below a pedestrian bridge, across the channel, and out onto a two-lane residential street. They are near homes now, and that can mean trouble. If dogs bark, the Border Patrol will suspect intruders.

Two cars pass. Panting and out of breath, they scuttle behind bushes. Half a block ahead is a red Chevrolet Blazer with tinted windows. The car flashes its headlights.

"Let's go," El Tiríndaro says.

As they reach the Chevy, locks click open. Enrique and the others scramble inside. In front sit a Latino driver and a woman passenger.

PUFFS OF CLOUDS

It is four a.m. Enrique is exhausted. He climbs onto pillows in the back of the Chevy. They feel like puffs of clouds. The engine starts. Enrique smiles to himself as though in a dream.

He can hardly believe he is in the United States of America.

The driver and the woman are members of El Tiríndaro's smuggling network. They pop open beers. For a moment,

Enrique worries: What if the driver has too many? He doesn't say anything. The Blazer heads toward Dallas.

The ceiling of the car blurs as Enrique's eyes close into sleep.

Now they are half a mile away from a Border Patrol checkpoint. Border Patrol agents pay special attention to bigger cars like SUVs and vans that can carry more migrants. Some smugglers strip out the backseats and stack the migrants like cordwood, one on top of another. Headlights tilted up mean more people in the back, weighing down the vehicle. Some smugglers favor windowless vans. When the agents notice anything suspicious—like a car weaving slightly because it is loaded up—they pull alongside and shine a flashlight into the eyes of the passengers. If the riders do not look over but seem frozen in their seats, they are likely to be illegal immigrants. Enrique sleeps soundly until El Tiríndaro shakes him. "Get up!" El Tiríndaro says. The Blazer stops for them to get out. Enrique and the two Mexicans, with El Tiríndaro leading, climb a fence and walk east, away from the freeway. Then they turn north, parallel to it. Enrique can see the checkpoint at a distance.

Every car must stop. "U.S. citizens?" agents ask. Usually they check for documents.

Enrique and his group walk ten minutes more, then turn back toward the freeway. Overhead, he can see the first light of dawn. They crouch next to a billboard, waiting.

The Blazer pulls up. Enrique gets in and sinks back into the pillows. He thinks: I have crossed the last big hurdle. Never has he felt so happy. He recalls being high on glue and marijuana, and the inevitable crash that came after. No drug has ever given him what he feels now. He drifts back into a deep, blissful sleep.

Four hundred miles later, Enrique awakens. The Blazer has pulled into a gas station on the outskirts of Dallas. El Tiríndaro is gone. He has left without saying good-bye. Enrique feels a slight pang of sadness. It was comforting to be in this new land with someone he trusted. He does not know the driver. Enrique knows that El Tiríndaro gets a hundred dollars a client. Enrique's mother, Lourdes, has promised twelve hundred. The driver is the boss; he gets most of the money. El Tiríndaro is on his way back to Mexico.

The Blazer rolls into Dallas at about noon. America looks beautiful. The buildings are huge. The freeways are nothing like the dirt streets at home. Everything is clean.

After the driver drops off the Mexican siblings, he takes Enrique to a large house. There is a room filled with bags of clothing, in various sizes and American styles. The driver explains that he has them for migrants to change into so they will blend in. He tells Enrique to pick some new clothes to wear.

The smugglers focus on business: exchanging the money they are owed for Enrique. They telephone his mother.

LOURDES

Lourdes, now thirty-five years old, has come to love North Carolina. People are polite. There are plenty of jobs for immigrants, and it seems to be safe. Her daughter Diana quickly masters English.

It's been eleven years since Lourdes has seen the two children she left in Honduras, but she is always thinking about them. When Lourdes walks by stores that sell things they might like, she thinks of Enrique and Belky. When she sees a child Enrique's age, she tells herself, *Así debe estar mi muchachito.* My little boy must be this big now.

A small gray album holds treasures and painful memories: pictures of Belky, her daughter back home. At seven, Belky wears a white First Communion dress and long white gloves; at nine, a yellow cheerleader's skirt; at fifteen, for her *quinceañera,* a pink taffeta dress with lace sleeves and white satin shoes. Belky leans over a two-layer cake topped with white frosting and a pink angel. Lourdes spent seven hundred dollars to make the party special. She remembers how many hours she had to work to make that money. She promised Belky she would try to make it back to Honduras for the big event somehow. "I wanted to go. I wanted to go . . . ," Lourdes says. At eighteen, Belky wears a blue gown and mortarboard for her high school graduation.

There are pictures of Enrique, too: at eight in a tank top, with four piglets at his feet; at thirteen in the photograph at Belky's *quinceañera,* the serious-looking little brother. She most treasures a photo of her son in a pink shirt. It is the only one she has where he is smiling.

Lourdes has worried about her boy from afar. A year ago, in 1999, her sister in Honduras told her the truth about

Enrique: "He's getting in trouble. He's changed." The news that Enrique was taking drugs made her sick. Now that she knows the dangerous journey he is on, she is more worried than ever.

When Lourdes would telephone Honduras, she would tell Enrique to be patient. They would reunite soon, she promised. Now he is on his way. She is happy she will see her son, but anxious because they have been so distant for so long.

Lourdes has not slept. She has spent part of the night in her kitchen, praying before a tall candle that has the image of San Judas Tadeo, the saint who tackles difficult, even life-and-death, situations. All night, since Enrique's last call from a pay phone across the Rio Grande, she has been having visions of him floating on the river, drowned. She tells her boyfriend, "My greatest fear is never to see him again."

The phone rings. A female smuggler is on the other end. She says: We have your son in Texas, but $1,200 is not enough. We want $1,700.

Lourdes grows suspicious. Maybe Enrique is dead, and the smugglers are trying to cash in. "Put him on the line," she demands. How can she trust them for sure?

He's out shopping for food, the smuggler replies. Lourdes will not be put off.

He's asleep, the smuggler says.

How can he be both? Lourdes insists on talking to him.

Finally, the smuggler gives the phone to Enrique.

"*¿Sos tú?* Is it you?" his mother asks anxiously.

"*Sí, Mami,* it's me," she hears him say.

Still, Lourdes is not certain it is him. After all, she has heard his voice only a handful of times in eleven years.

"*¿Sos tú?*" she asks again. She grasps for something, any-thing, that she can ask this boy—a question that no one but Enrique can answer. She remembers what he told her about his shoes when he called on the pay phone.

"What kind of shoes do you have on?" she asks.

"Two left shoes," Enrique says.

Fear drains from his mother like a wave going back into the sea. It *is* Enrique. She feels pure happiness.

She wires the money to Dallas.

Enrique changes into the clean clothes and shoes the smug-glers gave him. The smugglers take him to a restaurant. He eats chicken smothered in cream sauce. Washed and well fed in his mother's adopted country, he is happy.

The smugglers drive him to a branch of Western Union, a company that can instantly transfer cash from one person to another. But there is no money under his mother's name, not even a message.

How could she do this? At worst, Enrique figures, he can break away. Run. But the smugglers keep an eye on him. They call his mother again.

Lourdes says she has sent the money through a female im-migrant who lives with her, because the woman gets a discount at the bank. The money should be there under the woman's name.

It is.

But there isn't time to celebrate.

The smugglers explain to Enrique that they will be leaving him with another smuggler in their network. They leave Enrique at a gas station and Enrique runs to get into a green van. There are four other migrants in the back of the van. They leave Texas and head for Orlando, Florida.

To Enrique, traveling by car feels like a luxury.

LOST AND FOUND

Lourdes's boyfriend has taken time off from work to drive to Orlando, where Enrique is waiting for him to arrive.

"Are you Lourdes's son?" the boyfriend asks.

Enrique looks up. He instantly recognizes the boyfriend's kind, handsome face from a video someone brought back to Honduras after visiting Lourdes in the United States.

Enrique nods.

They say little in the car. Enrique falls asleep.

By eight a.m. on May 28, Enrique is in North Carolina.

He wakes up in a panic. "Are we lost?" he asks. "Are you sure we aren't lost? Do you know where we are going?"

"We're almost there," Lourdes's boyfriend assures him gently.

They are driving fast down freshly paved roads, through pines and elms, past billboards and fields, yellow lilies and purple lilacs. The car goes over a bridge and passes cattle pastures with large rolls of hay. At the end of a short gravel road, there are house trailers. One is beige with white metal awnings. It is framed by tall green trees.

At ten a.m., after 122 days and more than 12,000 miles—including the seven futile attempts to get to his mother—Enrique, eleven years older than when she left him behind, bounds from the backseat of the car and up five faded redwood steps, and swings open the white door of the mobile home.

To the left, beyond a tiny living room, sits a girl with shoulder-length black hair and curly bangs. She is at the kitchen table eating breakfast. He remembers a picture of her. His sister Diana. She is nine now.

Enrique leans over and kisses her on the cheek.

"Are you my brother?" she asks.

He nods. "Where's my mother? Where's my mother?"

Diana motions past the kitchen to the far end of the trailer.

Enrique runs. He zigzags down two narrow hallways. He opens a door. Inside, the room is dark. On a queen-size bed, under a window draped with lace curtains, his mother is asleep. He jumps squarely onto the bed next to her. He gives her a hug. Then a kiss.

"You're here, *mi hijo*."

"I'm here," he says.

8

PERHAPS A NEW LIFE

At first, neither Enrique nor Lourdes cries. He kisses her cheek again. She holds him tight. He has played this out in his mind a thousand times. It is just as he thought it would be.

All day they talk. He tells her about his travels: the assault on top of a train, leaping off to save his life, the hunger, thirst, and fear. He has lost 28 pounds and is down to 107. He feels fragile in her embrace. His bruises and scars frighten her. Her instinct is to hug him, feed him, nurture him. She cooks him rice, beans, and fried pork and watches with pleasure as he eats.

The boy she last saw when he was in kindergarten is now taller than she is. He has her nose, her round face, her eyes, her curly hair. Lourdes has three children, but Enrique is special to her. He is her only son.

"Look, Mom, look what I put here." He pulls up his shirt. She sees a tattoo.

EnriqueLourdes, it says.

His mother winces. Tattoos, she says, are for delinquents, for people in jail. "I'm going to tell you, son, I don't like this." She pauses. "But at least if you had to get a tattoo, you remembered me."

"I've always remembered you."

He tells her about Honduras, how he sold the shoes and clothes she sent to buy glue, how he wanted to get away from drugs, how he ached to be with her. Finally, Lourdes cries.

She asks about Belky, her daughter in Honduras; her own mother; and the deaths of two of her brothers. Then she stops. She feels too guilty to go on.

Eight people live here. Several have left their children behind. All they have is pictures. Lourdes's boyfriend has two sons in Honduras. He has not seen them in five years. The trailer is awash in guilt.

Children like Enrique dream that when they finally find their mothers, they will live happily ever after. For weeks—months, even—the mothers and children hold on to a fairy-tale idea of how they should feel toward one another. Then their true feelings surface. The children say they resent having been left behind. They accuse their mothers of lying to them when they promised to quickly come back to their home countries or send for them. Now that the children are in the United States, their mothers are working hard and don't have time to make up for all the attention they missed out on while they were apart. Worse, jealousies grow when the children have to split their mother's attention with children she had in the United States.

The mothers demand respect from their children for the huge sacrifice they made coming to the United States so their children back home could eat and study. They worked hard, and lived lonely lives away from their families and children. When their children accuse them of abandoning them, the mothers think they are just ungrateful brats.

As they spend time together, mothers and children discover just how far apart they are.

NEWS FROM THE UNITED STATES

In Honduras, Enrique's grandmother Águeda walks next door to find María Isabel at her aunt Gloria's house.

She has news: Enrique is in the United States. He has made it to Lourdes's house.

María Isabel wails, "He's not coming back!" She locks herself in her bedroom and cries for two hours. Will they even see each other again? At night, Gloria can still hear her sobbing.

For the next few months, María Isabel spends hours at a time silently sitting on a rock in front of the house.

"Cheer up," Gloria's daughter tells María Isabel. "He's there. He'll send money. If he'd stayed, you would both have died of hunger." But María Isabel, normally always giggling, is inconsolable.

Belky, too, is depressed. She stops talking. She cries every morning. Maybe, she tells herself, she should have gone with Enrique, taken the risk. Both he and Diana are with her mother. "Now I'm the only one left here," she tells Aunt Rosa Amalia in tears.

UNFAMILIAR TERRITORY

Enrique likes the people in the trailer, especially his mother's boyfriend. He thinks the boyfriend could be a much better father than his own dad.

Lourdes's boyfriend helps Enrique find work as a painter. With his first paycheck, Enrique offers to pick up $50 of the grocery bill. He buys Diana a gift: a pair of pink sandals for $5.97. He sends money to Belky and to María Isabel in Honduras.

Lourdes brags to her friends: "This is my son. Look at him! He's so big. It's a miracle he's here."

Whenever he leaves the house, she hugs him. When she comes home from work, they sit on the couch, watching her favorite soap opera, with her hand resting on his arm. Each Sunday, they go shopping together to buy enough food to last the week. Lourdes cooks for Enrique, and he starts gaining weight.

But in time, Lourdes and Enrique discover they hardly know each other. Neither is familiar with the other's likes or dislikes. They haven't seen each other in over a decade. They are strangers.

At first, Enrique is quiet and shy around the house. As he

settles in, he begins to change. He goes to a pool hall without asking permission. Occasionally, he curses. Lourdes tells him not to. Enrique plans to work painting houses to make money. His mother wants him to study English, prepare for a profession.

"*¡No, Mami!*" he says. "No one is going to change me."

With others, Enrique is openly affectionate, especially with his half sister, Diana. He gives her money, drives her to the store, plays piggyback with her, gives her hugs. He teaches her to dance. They play rhymes together. She is happy to have a big brother.

With his mother, he is on edge. Their fights are often sparked by Lourdes's scolding. Don't drink and drive, she tells him. Control your drinking. Be more careful with money. You can't spend a thousand dollars as if it were ten. Lourdes blames Enrique's grandmother María: she spoiled the boy and let him run wild. Lourdes is determined to impose discipline on her son. It is for his own sake, she says.

But Enrique cuts her off. He tells her she can't treat him like the little boy she left behind. He's grown up now. Didn't he fend for himself growing up? Didn't he hop freight trains across Mexico? "You keep sticking your nose into things that are none of your business!" Enrique tells Lourdes, adding that she should just shut up and leave him alone.

"You will respect me when I talk to you!" Lourdes yells back. "I am your mother." She walks up behind him and spanks him hard on his buttocks, several times.

"You have no right to hit me! You didn't raise me." He tells her that only his grandmother María, who raised him, has that right.

Lourdes disagrees. "I sent money. I supported you. That is raising you!"

Enrique locks himself in the bathroom and sobs. He throws around anything he can find—toothpaste, shampoo, a perfume bottle. Diana hides in the bedroom, crying. Lourdes's boyfriend tries to calm her.

Enrique storms out of the house. Lourdes's boyfriend and his cousin cruise the streets, trying to find him. Enrique hides behind a small church two miles away. He sleeps in the graveyard behind the church, between the headstones. The graveyard brings back haunting memories. He recalls lying flat atop a mausoleum back in Chiapas, frantically praying police would not catch him. Now he awakens surrounded by crickets and dewy grass and a different worry. He feels guilty for storming out on his mother. He wonders if he was just testing his mother's love, testing to see if she'd follow him.

Lourdes stays up most of the night. She knows he is just punishing her, making her nervous, and that he will be back. But what, she worries, will their future together be like if they are already fighting? Will they always argue this much? It seems as though the anger Enrique felt toward her for leaving has not faded over time, it has only piled up. She expected Enrique to love her like the five-year-old who clung to her in Honduras. She has been a good person, a good mother. Why is God punishing her?

The next afternoon, their love prevails. Enrique ducks into

the trailer and apologizes to his mother for storming out and scaring her. He tells Lourdes he loves her. He comforts her with a little white lie. He tells her he spent the night safely sleeping in her car.

They share hugs and kisses. That night, they watch soap operas together on the living room sofa. As they sit side by side, Lourdes can feel her son's love.

A NEW LIFE

When Enrique phones Honduras, he learns María Isabel is pregnant, as he suspected before he left. On November 2, 2000, she gives birth to their daughter.

She and Enrique name the baby Katerin Jasmín. The baby looks like him. She has his mouth, his nose, his eyes. An aunt urges María Isabel to go to the United States, alone. The aunt promises to take care of the baby.

"If I have the opportunity, I'll go," María Isabel says. "I'll leave my baby behind."

Enrique agrees. "We'll have to leave the baby behind."

9

THE GIRL LEFT BEHIND

Enrique knows he does not hate his mother. But with each passing day, his resentment grows. After months with Lourdes, he can no longer contain it. One day he snaps. He goes on a tirade.

He tells Lourdes she didn't care enough about her children to stay with them in Honduras. Did she think sending money could substitute for being at his side? Or mend the loneliness he felt being moved from one relative to the next? "Money doesn't solve anything," he tells her.

He yells at Lourdes for leaving him with a father she knew was irresponsible. Why didn't she put him with her own family, who cared for his sister Belky? Why didn't she send enough money so he wouldn't have to sell spices when he was only ten?

"How could I ask you for anything?" he tells Lourdes. "I

would go a year without talking to you." He accuses her of playing favorites, of sending Belky money to cover tuition at a private school her aunt sent her to. "Belky always got more from you," he says. "Belky is going to be a professional. Look at me," he says. He wanted to study, he insists, he just didn't want to have to beg his mother for the money.

Nothing, he tells her, was gained by their long separation. "People come here to prosper. You have nothing here. What have you accomplished?" He is on a roll. He is so mad he wants to hurt her feelings.

If she had stayed in Honduras, he shouts, he would have turned out better. "I wouldn't be this way if I had had two parents."

Why did she continually promise to return for Christmas and then never show up? Once she knew he was in trouble sniffing glue, he asks her, how could she stay away? "You left me, abandoned me," he tells her. He berates his mother for what he sees as her biggest mistake: "You shouldn't have gotten pregnant until you knew your existing kids were okay."

A true mother, he tells Lourdes, isn't the person who carries you in her womb. It is someone who raises and nurtures you. He tells her his true mother is his grandmother María. He misses the beans and spaghetti she made for him. He misses how she sang "Happy Birthday" for him every year.

Then Enrique lands the most hurtful blow. He plans to leave her and return to Honduras in two years. "I'm not going to do the same as you—stay here all my life."

Lourdes is stunned. Her heart fills with guilt and hurt.

She must show Enrique he is terribly mistaken. "What about the money I sent you?" she says. Whenever he asked for something—a television, a soccer ball—she sent it. Belky got more money only because Aunt Rosa Amalia insisted Lourdes pay for Belky to go to private school.

Lourdes tells him about the struggles she, too, endured during their years apart. For the first time, she admits to the extreme poverty and humiliating circumstances she lived through. She tells him about working as a *fichera* in a bar, surrounded by drunk men; about cleaning for wealthy people who mocked her; about being fiercely independent and hard-working so she could pay for her three children's health and happiness. "I killed myself trying to help you," she says, exasperated.

She's not like some mothers she knows who leave Honduras and forget their children, never call, never write. I called. I wrote, she tells her son. Blame your father. He promised to take care of you while I was away. He abandoned you. Your father's family had an equal responsibility to provide for your needs. Instead, Lourdes continues—she, too, is on a roll—your grandmother María sent you to sell spices in the market, where you learned about drugs.

"You are what you are because you didn't want to study," she adds. "It's not my fault. I wanted you to study. You preferred to be on drugs." Had she sent more money, Lourdes tells Enrique, he would have just spent it on drugs.

Lourdes thinks of how her own mother couldn't provide enough food for her children. At the age of eight, Lourdes sought out odd jobs. A neighbor gave her clothes to wash in the river twice a week. When she was nine, her mother dispatched her and Rosa Amalia, then ten, to work as live-in maids. Lourdes had to quit elementary school. When she was fourteen, her mother sent her to live with her brother Marco, in southern Honduras.

"My mother is sacred to me. I thank her for the little she did for us," Lourdes says. She tells him he is an ungrateful brat. She says God will punish him for the way he is acting. Someday, she adds, your daughter will treat you the way you now treat me.

"Shut up. Leave me in peace!" he yells.

Day after day, they argue. Enrique loves to contradict his mother, to set her off, even when he knows she is right. He thinks it is terribly funny to see her get mad. At dinner, he burps loudly and doesn't excuse himself. He slams doors and blasts music. He talks over her to annoy her. He leaves his clothes and shoes strewn about the living room, and doesn't bother helping clear his place after dinner. When he goes out at night, he refuses to tell Lourdes where.

For Enrique, alcohol is an escape from the fights. Almost all of the men on his paint crew, depressed to be away from their home countries, are big drinkers. From Thursday through Sunday, in the evenings, he goes to a local bar, with a dark, low-slung ceiling, four pool tables, a long bar, and a jukebox that plays Latino music. He starts going to a discotheque and spending money on drinks and lap dances. After going out, Enrique doesn't have enough money to pay Lourdes his share of the bills. He isn't sending as much money to María Isabel and their baby as he could.

Most of the time, he goes to bed at one a.m., drunk, and gets up at six a.m. for work.

Enrique is breaking a promise he made to himself to leave his addictions behind once he crossed into the United States. But he feels abnormal, as if he were crawling out of his skin, if he isn't drunk or high.

At least he's not sniffing glue.

Enrique maintains one ritual. Each Sunday, he telephones María Isabel in Honduras.

She waits for his call at the home of one of Lourdes's cousins. When she answers the telephone, she is so overcome with emotion she cannot speak.

"María Isabel, say something, anything," Enrique pleads.

"I miss you. I love you. Don't forget me," she says, crying.

He starts trying to send her one hundred dollars or more a month. He vows he will be back in Honduras within two years and together they will raise Jasmín.

HOLIDAYS

Winter comes. Enrique's family and others who share the trailer move into a newer, three-bedroom duplex. It has a big kitchen and a living room with three sofas draped in lilac floral slipcovers. There is enough space to hang a painting of the Virgin of Guadalupe, a wooden carving of the map of Honduras, and a small American flag. Still, the home is crowded.

Until now, Enrique has never returned to his worst vice: sniffing glue. A few days before Christmas, beer and marijuana are no longer enough. He ends the workday by pouring a little paint thinner into an empty soda can, hoping to get high off the fumes. He brings the can home. He does the same the next night. The thinner doesn't give him as good a high as Honduran glue, but it's handy.

Even in the larger duplex home, there is little room for Enrique to hide his bad habits. One night, as he heads out to meet his friends, Lourdes notices he is hiding something under his arm.

"What do you have there? Show me," Lourdes says from the living room sofa.

Enrique brushes past her. "None of your business," he says.

Lourdes jumps up and grabs him by the shirt. She smells paint thinner. She knows what the smell means.

"You're broken, ruined. A drug addict! Why did you even come here? To finish screwing yourself up?" Lourdes's words tumble out. She doesn't care that her boyfriend and three of his relatives are in the living room, listening.

Enrique shakes himself loose. He curses her.

"You're a disgrace," she tells him. "Get your act together!" If he keeps sniffing paint thinner, Lourdes tells him he has to move out. She must think of her daughter. She doesn't want Diana exposed to drugs.

Enrique does not respond. He peels out of the gravel driveway in his truck.

Lourdes is despondent. She worries that he will kill himself driving recklessly. For the first time in her life, Lourdes feels like she wants to die. Maybe if she were gone, she tells herself, Enrique would know what it is truly like not to have a mother.

Enrique knows that his body cannot withstand the paint thinner. Each time he inhales the fumes, the left side of his head, where he took the worst of the beating on top of the train, aches badly. His left eyelid, which still droops slightly from the assault, pulses and twitches. He has excruciating pain when he turns his head.

He stops sniffing. He's not stopping because his mother wants him to, he insists, he is doing it for himself.

Lourdes prepares for her first Christmas reunited with Enrique. She has grown to dread the holiday. Each Christmas without her children, she cried and became more hard-hearted. She wished the holidays would never arrive.

This year, paying Enrique's smuggler has left her strapped for money. She puts up a small plastic Christmas tree. She crowds it with ornaments. Enrique tells her it is ugly. On Christmas Eve, Enrique ignores the family and goes out drinking with friends. He comes home late, and drunk. The next morning, Lourdes gives her son a shirt. Enrique doesn't have a gift for his mother. She is hurt.

Enrique cannot shake how many Christmases he feels she has ruined for him, leaving him waiting and never showing up. Now he wants to ruin her holiday.

New Year's Eve is better. Lourdes has never celebrated New Year's Eve in the United States. It brings back too many memories of Honduras, where she would run home from a party at midnight to hug her mother. This year, Lourdes goes to a party with Enrique. At midnight, she kisses her son. Enrique hugs her back, hard. "Happy New Year. I love you," he tells his mother. For the first time in all her years in the United States, Lourdes doesn't cry on New Year's Eve.

NEWS FROM HONDURAS

Enrique's family starts criticizing María Isabel. His aunts say that Jasmín is barefoot, dirty, and badly dressed. They say that she is skinny and pale and often has a cough. If Enrique sends money, they complain, why doesn't María Isabel take Jasmín to a good private doctor, not the public clinic?

María Isabel spends most of the money on Jasmín. She also gives fifteen dollars a month to Aunt Gloria. She stocks Gloria's refrigerator with fruit, milk, and chicken. She sends ten dollars across town to her mother to help her buy heart and asthma medicine.

Enrique's aunts and sister next door tell María Isabel she is spending too much money on her family, and not enough on Enrique's daughter. María Isabel is enraged, but she says nothing. María Isabel has spent most of her life deprived of decent clothing. Can't she buy a dress or splurge $2.50 to get her hair dyed? She cannot live with her aunt Gloria without giving her some help, too.

She is grateful for the little Enrique sends. Still, it is not enough.

Enrique's aunt Mirian is angry she doesn't have enough income to feed her three children well or send them to school, while at the same time all of Enrique's money is going to the girl next door. She sends him a letter about María Isabel. She reports, simply, that María Isabel isn't being a good mother and is misspending his money.

On the phone, he scolds María Isabel: "If you don't take good care of that girl, I will have to ask my family to take her away from you!"

For a moment, María Isabel is silent. Then her voice turns stiff. "No one takes my daughter away from me."

María Isabel has come to hate Enrique's family. One day, after too many criticisms from them, she offers up Jasmín. "Here she is. Take her! You can raise her. Let Enrique send money to you," she yells over to Enrique's family. "If the dollars are causing you to make all of these allegations, keep the damn dollars!" She decides to move away from them and return to her mother's tiny wooden hut, which clings to a mountainside in a neighborhood called Los Tubos. The mud trail up to the hut is so steep that María Isabel has to grab the roots of a large rubber tree to climb up to the hut's door. Nine people sleep inside. While María Isabel is at work, both her mother, Eva, and her younger sister will help care for Jasmín, who is now one and a half years old. She does not give Enrique's family an address where she can be reached.

María Isabel's family, among the poorest in Los Tubos, eats twice a day. They have no refrigerator. They cook on two small burners. All that has kept disaster away has been María

Isabel's oldest sister, who sends money from Texas, where she lives. Most children in the neighborhood don't go on to junior high because reaching the nearest school requires bus fare. Men work as bricklayers; women clean houses in wealthy neighborhoods.

Still, María Isabel's life gets better.

Six days a week, at eleven a.m., María Isabel sets out for her new job at a children's clothing store at the Mall Multiplaza downtown.

There, salesgirls ask María Isabel to fetch shoes of a certain style and size from the back of the store. She shoves the box through a small opening in the wall. The light-filled mall, where Tegucigalpa's wealthy shop, has beige marble floors, potted palms, air-conditioning, and glass elevators.

She gets home at ten p.m. The job pays $120 a month.

Jasmín plays with her dolls and gives them baths. She chases her grandmother's black-and-white chicks, making them scurry across the kitchen floor. She plays dress-up with the little girl next door, or *agua de limón,* where they lock hands and swing each other around in circles.

Each day, the girl reminds María Isabel more and more of Enrique. Like him, she stands slightly knock-kneed, her pelvis thrust out, her bottom tucked under. She has his deep, raspy voice. She has the same temperament as Enrique and Lourdes: she is testy, a stubborn fighter who stands her ground.

When Jasmín turns two, María Isabel takes her to talk to her father on the telephone at an Internet store. María Isabel knows his number by heart.

She sits before the gray computer, and Jasmín stands between her legs. "Mom, pass the phone," Jasmín demands, reaching for the computer headset. Often, the things Jasmín tells her father are lines that María Isabel has told her to say. Jasmín returns to her grandmother's and proudly announces, "I spoke with my daddy, Enrique."

"They are strangers," Eva says to María Isabel, "but they are blood."

Eva often shows Jasmín the photos Enrique has sent of himself. She tells Jasmín that someday she will go in an airplane to see her father. Jasmín figures her father must have left on an airplane, too. Whenever she hears one in the sky, she stops what she is doing and races outside. She looks up, her eyes bright. She thrusts both arms up and waves madly. *"¡Adiós, Papi Enrique!"* she yells.

NO REGRETS

Enrique has been living in the United States for nearly two and a half years. He is wound up tight. He's working at a company that pushes everyone to paint excessively fast. He comes home exhausted and cranky.

Lourdes is sick of their arguing and of the guilt that drove her to spoil Enrique after he first arrived. She packed his lunch, cooked his dinner, dropped off his truck payments. She asked herself repeatedly: Would he have turned out differently if she hadn't left him?

She can tell he is going out of his way to make her mad, so

she forces herself to be more distant. If Enrique does something she doesn't like, she tries hard to ignore it. She stops doing his laundry. They no longer routinely go out to dinner on Saturday night or grocery shopping on Sunday.

One evening, Lourdes and her boyfriend are watching a soap opera on the living room television. In the kitchen the next room over, Enrique and a friend are playing cards. Each time they slap a card down, they yell.

Lourdes walks into the kitchen. She looks cross. "What are you doing?" she demands.

"If you don't want noise, you should live alone," he says without looking up from the game.

"You're an ignoramus," she answers.

Lourdes goes back to the television. Enrique and his friend slap the cards down harder and harder.

Lourdes stomps into the kitchen. Her boyfriend knows trouble is near. He soon follows.

"Be quiet!" she orders. "You must respect me. Don't forget, I am your mother. I gave birth to you."

"I don't love you as if you were my mother. I love my grandmother."

"I gave birth to you."

"That's not my fault!"

Lourdes grabs Enrique's shirt around the shoulders. Enrique pushes his chair back and bolts up. Lourdes slaps him on the mouth, hard. Enrique grabs her two hands, near her neck, to prevent further blows. Lourdes assumes that he is trying to grab her throat. "Let go of me!" she screams.

Lourdes's boyfriend pulls them apart. Then he ushers Enrique outside. Enrique is crying.

This argument feels like the last straw. There are no words of regret.

They have all grown sick of the fighting in the cramped duplex. It is a toxic environment for Diana to grow up in. Enrique decides to move out and rent a bedroom in a trailer.

Paying his own rent means spending money in the United States that he would otherwise send back home. Rent on his share of the trailer and utilities is $280. Between payments for his truck, gas, his cell phone, and food, he is running low on cash. He's had to pay two police tickets. Sometimes, when work is slow, Lourdes has to loan him money.

Enrique had been sending María Isabel money monthly. But in the past year, he has wired money only four times, usually between $150 and $180.

Enrique is too embarrassed to tell María Isabel he is struggling with money, and he doesn't want her to know how much he is wasting on beer. She wonders if he is sending his daughter less money because he is spending it on another girlfriend. Enrique swears that there is no one else.

Still, it feels like their relationship is coming undone.

Friends warn María Isabel: We know you adore Enrique, but don't grow old waiting for him. If he doesn't send for you or return to Honduras soon, find someone else before you get too old and lose your looks.

Right after Enrique left, María Isabel felt desperate to be with him again. Over time, she has adapted to his absence.

When they speak on the telephone, she cries less. She has matured, changed. Now her life revolves around her daughter.

"I love him," she says, "but not like before."

María Isabel has heard that Enrique drinks too much. She knows his history with drugs and wonders if she can believe him when he says he has stopped taking them.

Equally troubling: Enrique calls less frequently. She feels snubbed. It feels as though the phone calls have become a one-way street. She is tired of spending the morning on Sunday, her one day off, downtown at the Internet store dialing Enrique. She stops calling.

Enrique no longer talks of returning to Honduras. He says he likes the comforts of the United States.

He hasn't hired a smuggler to bring her to him in the States because she hasn't asked for one. She hasn't said yes to coming because he hasn't hired a smuggler. The less frequently they talk, the less they understand each other. Both are stuck in their pride.

PROGRESS

With his third New Year's Day in the United States, Enrique resolves to change. He realizes he can no longer wallow in what happened in the past. He's not hurting his mother as much as he is hurting himself.

Drinking so much alcohol makes his stomach ache constantly. He's tired of going to work nauseous after spending all night out drinking. He tells friends he'll quit beer and drugs altogether when María Isabel is at his side. He hopes to bring her next year and get married.

He cuts his hair short and loses the weight he has gained from beer. He wishes he could get rid of the scars on his forehead and his knees, the bump under the skin by his left eye, the pain in his teeth anytime he eats anything hot or cold. Maybe he can at least get caps put on his broken teeth.

He stops playing his music loud and slamming doors. When he burps, he excuses himself. On Saturday nights, he and Lourdes watch the Spanish-language variety show *Sábado Gigante* together, as they did when he first arrived.

Enrique starts working seven days a week. Bit by bit, he cuts back on beer and marijuana. He used to go out three or more times a week; now it's just once or twice a month to play pool. He drinks a few beers, then switches to soda. When friends invite him to party, he tells them he's not interested anymore.

Most important, he decides he has to be more responsible for Jasmín. He can't have her grow up worrying about money as he did. He wants her to study. He can no longer blow hundreds of dollars in a single night of partying or thousands on troubles with the police. That has been a huge waste of money.

If he doesn't change, he will repeat his mother's mistake; time will slip by, and Jasmín will grow up without him. He must save fifty thousand dollars as quickly as possible to buy a house and start a business in Honduras.

Nearly every day, Enrique sees things Jasmín might like—candy, toys, dresses. He tells himself he would buy them for her if she were there. He talks about her constantly to his friends.

He didn't like school. He worries: Will she be the same?

His happiest moments are when photographs arrive. In his bedroom, Enrique tapes two pictures of his daughter to his mirror, and keeps two more on the shelf by his bed. He loves it when María Isabel puts Jasmín on the line. *"Te quiero, Papi,"* Jasmín says. "I love you, Daddy." He knows María Isabel prompts Jasmín to say nice things to him. He doesn't care. I think she'll love me when she sees me, he tells himself. He pictures how their lives together will be. Everyone in Lourdes's home eats dinner at a different hour. They all eat whenever they get home from work. His family will eat dinner all together.

MOTHERHOOD

The more attached María Isabel becomes to Jasmín, the more she resists leaving her. As Jasmín turns three, she is inseparable from her mother. At night, they sleep in the same bed. In the morning, before she readies herself for work, María Isabel bathes her daughter and braids her hair in pigtails.

When María Isabel heads off to work, Jasmín is in tears. *"Mami! Mami!"* she cries, scrambling after her barefoot.

"*Ya vuelvo.* I'll be right back," María Isabel calls up the hill as she walks away, waving.

At night, Jasmín sits on María Isabel's lap. They rub noses and play patty-cake. María Isabel teaches Jasmín how to count. With each number, she bounces Jasmín on her lap and the girl squeals with delight.

On María Isabel's day off, she and Jasmín walk downtown, where the streets are crowded with carts piled with potatoes, plantains, and avocados. It is where Lourdes once sold gum and candy from a little box with Enrique at her side. María Isabel carries Jasmín in her arms to the city's central plaza, where children beg with outstretched arms. She takes her into the cathedral, up to the gilded altar. She prays. She asks that Jasmín not get sick, that Enrique stay away from drugs. Then she takes Jasmín for a scoop of ice cream.

At dusk they take a bus home, Jasmín in María Isabel's arms. Lights twinkle on the hills of Tegucigalpa. María Isabel undresses Jasmín and slips on her white nightgown.

At seven-thirty p.m., María Isabel climbs into bed with her daughter. Jasmín holds a bottle of milk with her left hand. With her right hand, she rubs her mother's belly. It is a ritual. She cannot fall asleep without stroking her mother's belly. Slowly, as she sucks on the milk, Jasmín loses her grip on the bottle. Her eyelids flutter. María Isabel rolls her over. She rubs Jasmín's back until the girl falls asleep.

María Isabel can no longer imagine leaving her daughter. At most, she might leave Jasmín when the girl is old enough to understand what is happening. "She would have to be at least five years old for me to leave her. Then, at least, I could try to explain it to her," María Isabel tells her family. Not a day before, she says firmly. It is the same age Enrique was when his mother left.

Some of her friends tell her she would be a fool not to follow Enrique to the United States. She is young and can find work now, but the older she gets, the harder it will be for her to find a job here. In Honduras, many employers won't hire women who are any older than twenty-five. María Isabel sees job advertisements that say they will only hire women up to that age.

There are factories across Tegucigalpa that hire young women to sit in rows behind sewing machines. The women stitch clothes that will be shipped to the United States; they may repeat the same motions over the sewing machines more than twenty-five hundred times a day, forty-four hours a week, for $110 a month. Employers assume that by the age of thirty, women will work more slowly and get less done. They might develop back or eye problems or arthritis from the demanding physical labor. The employers want to hire only women who can keep up the grueling pace.

The children's clothing store María Isabel works at won't hire women older than twenty-three. Middle-aged women have three options, says María Isabel's neighbor: washing and ironing clothes, cleaning houses, or making tortillas at home, jobs that pay $50 to $90 a month. Social workers note that a family needs $350 a month minimum.

Good, reliable jobs go to people in certain families or with connections. Most of María Isabel's neighbors have no work. They survive only because someone in the family has gone north and sends back money. Single mothers and their children tend to suffer the most.

María Isabel's sister Irma tried to make it to the United States but ran out of money in Mexico and had to turn back. So did one of her brothers. María Isabel asks her sister about her trip. Irma tells her she was often hungry. María Isabel asks if she was raped. Irma looks away and doesn't answer.

María Isabel fears the same thing would happen to her. And what if she doesn't make it at all? What would become of Jasmín?

And if she did make it to the United States, she'd have to live there illegally, always fearful of being caught and deported. She would face racism; she would be treated as inferior, different. She has heard that the United States is a cold place, where neighbors barely know one another.

She doesn't want to miss all the important moments in Jasmín's life. She thinks about everything Enrique has already missed. Soon Jasmín will attend her first day of kindergarten.

María Isabel has heard how mothers who leave lose the love of their children. Enrique and Lourdes, she knows, still struggle with this. She devises a plan to stay. She will work hard, not have any more children, and therefore be able to provide Jasmín with a good education.

"I'm not leaving without Jasmín," María Isabel tells her aunt Gloria.

A DAUGHTER LEFT BEHIND

Belky begins to think that if she doesn't see her mother soon, she will never see her. "I just want to give her a hug. A bunch of hugs. I just want to be by her side—even if it's for a short while," she says.

When she finishes her college studies in business administration, she hopes to eventually form her own family in Honduras. Belky has started dating a new boyfriend, Yovani. One night Yovani proposes as they sit outside her cinder-block hut. Yovani is not handsome. He lives with his mother, a tamale maker, in a tiny wooden shack. But he is kind, he rarely drinks, and he treats her like a queen. She loves him. Belky asks Lourdes to provide a few thousand dollars to build a little house on land beside her grandmother's home—land reserved for the house Lourdes was to build upon her return. When she marries, her mother won't be there. Her aunt and uncle will walk her down the aisle.

When Belky was growing up, night after night she had the same prayer. She would ask God to let her see her mother again. She told God she would be satisfied even if she only saw and hugged her mother once more. Belky doesn't tell Lourdes, but she has given up on her prayer. She has lost any hope of ever seeing her mother again. She will not allow herself to even imagine what a reunion might be like.

She has an education. She has a partner who supports her and loves her. That, she decides, is where her future rests.

ANOTHER MOVE

In North Carolina, Lourdes works on a cleaning crew, then on a factory assembly line. It is hard, living with so many people jammed into their home. The men don't help with what they consider to be "women's work." When Lourdes arrives home from a full day's work, the kitchen trash container is full, the floors are dirty, and she must cook and clean for everyone.

Although the men come home at different hours, Lourdes waits up to serve each of them dinner. On her day off, she takes everyone's laundry—six baskets—to the Laundromat, and she buys enough groceries to last them all a week. Having seven people split the cost of rent allows Lourdes to send money back to Belky and her mother, Grandmother Águeda, in Honduras. It seems as though every relative in Honduras who has money troubles thinks he or she can ask Lourdes for help.

With the new year, Lourdes, her boyfriend, and their housemates decide to leave North Carolina. The paint firm where most of the men work is in financial trouble and has cut back on everyone's hours. Jobs are scarce.

They move to Florida, where a cousin of Lourdes's boyfriend gets all the men painting jobs. Lourdes starts as a hotel maid for $6.50 an hour, cleaning sixteen to eighteen rooms per shift. Eight people cram into a small two-bedroom apartment. Enrique sleeps on the living room sofa. He hates it. He misses the friends he made in North Carolina. He has to get up before dawn to be painting by six-thirty a.m.

Lourdes wants to enjoy her life more and worry about Enrique less. She and her boyfriend go out Saturday nights to a buffet dinner. Lourdes relishes moments with her daughter Diana. She is proud that Diana is bilingual in English and

Spanish. She teases Diana when she flubs a phrase in Spanish. Diana helps teach her mother English with a southern drawl.

As time passes, Enrique slowly learns that his mother will never offer an apology for leaving him. He tries to put the love he has always felt for Lourdes above the resentment he has harbored all these years. He gives his mother his first gift: one hundred dollars for her birthday. She uses it to buy a dress and a bottle of lotion.

As he forgives her, he becomes more loving. "*Tan bonita mi mami, la quiero mucho.* My beautiful mother, I love you so much," he says.

Lourdes teases, "*¡Mentiroso viejo!* You old liar!"

Lourdes is sure that God is answering one of her prayers: that Enrique straighten up, stop drinking, and no longer feel so bitter toward her. "It's like a miracle," she says. It is as if all the hurt he felt inside had to come out and now he is ready to move on. She feels the same warmth and love from Enrique as when he first arrived on her doorstep in North Carolina.

"He always wanted to be with me," she says.

NO GOOD-BYES

It is spring 2004. Enrique has been gone from Honduras for four years.

Now Enrique fears that if he and María Isabel live apart too long, she will find someone else. "If you find someone who loves you as much as I do, go with him," Enrique says. "I left you. I understand." In truth, he doesn't mean it. He wants to hear her say that she isn't interested in anyone else, that she never will be.

María Isabel tells him she loves him for life.

He decides to ask point-blank: Then are you coming to the United States or not? He is scared of the answer, though. He knows María Isabel has been stalling, that she is anxious about leaving Jasmín. He's been stalling her arrival, too: he wants to learn English and completely stop using drugs and alcohol before she comes.

Time passes.

"Why don't you call me?" Enrique asks the next time they speak. María Isabel answers curtly that she doesn't have anything to talk about.

"Are you ready to come?" he asks. He tells her she has to make a decision now. He won't wait for her any longer.

"I don't want to leave," she admits. Even if she is serious about coming, she can't leave until Jasmín is at least five years old. She promised.

If you come, he tells her, it will be the best thing for Jasmín. Together, we'll provide her with a better life. We'll both be able to return to her sooner. I want to be with Jasmín by the time she is five, six at the latest. If not, he confesses, he is scared Jasmín won't embrace him as her father.

María Isabel wants Jasmín to have a father, too. Jasmín has taken to calling the only man in Eva's house, her twenty-seven-year-old uncle Miguel, *Papi*. When she is on the phone with Enrique, Jasmín has to be coached to talk. With Uncle Miguel, words of affection come naturally. Jasmín is generous with her uncle Miguel; she shares her treats and toys. Each night, she flops on his bed and chatters about her day. María Isabel hasn't told Enrique this because she knows it will hurt his feelings.

Enrique tries to sway María Isabel. "I've changed," he tells her. "I drink, but just a little now." He adds: "I'm not the same person."

Now she is listening. "I'll think about it," she says.

Her answer fills Enrique with hope.

I need you, he tells her. You're the mother of my child. You're the only one I want to marry. Come be with me in America.

Enrique misses her serene, calm nature. He also misses how much she would cry and giggle. He misses walking her home from school holding her hand.

Day and night, María Isabel turns it over in her mind. Would going to the United States really allow Jasmín to have both her parents at her side more quickly? If María Isabel stays in Honduras and marries someone else, her husband might never treat Jasmín as if she were his own.

María Isabel decides: In the long run, leaving will help Jasmín. Eventually, she will be with her real mother and father, everyone together. María Isabel strikes a deal with Enrique: Jasmín will live with Belky but spend weekends with Eva, María Isabel's mother.

I will do it for my daughter, she tells herself.

A few days later, a smuggler contacts María Isabel. He has been hired by Enrique. The smuggler says he will call next week, probably on Tuesday or Wednesday. She must be ready.

María Isabel hauls all of Jasmín's clothing and dolls over to

Belky's cinder-block hut. She hugs her daughter over and over. She cries and cries.

Jasmín asks, "Why are you crying so much, *Mami*?"

María Isabel tells Jasmín her arm hurts. She tells her a cavity in her tooth aches.

"Don't cry, *Mami*," Jasmín says. Saddened by her mother's tears, Jasmín cries, too.

She asks her mother why she has moved all her clothes from her grandmother Eva's to Belky's hut across town. Why, she asks her mother, has María Isabel packed a backpack with her own clothes?

María Isabel hasn't told her daughter she is leaving. She can't. María Isabel hates lying to Jasmín, but she is sure her daughter is too young, at three and a half, to understand the truth. Jasmín would demand to be taken along. María Isabel doesn't want to see her daughter cry. This is easier, better, she tells herself.

Wednesday. The smuggler calls at one p.m. María Isabel must be across town, at Tegucigalpa's main bus station, at three-thirty p.m. The smuggler says he will be wearing a red shirt and blue jeans.

María Isabel's heart races. She holds Jasmín in her arms and gives her a last bottle of milk.

María Isabel hugs her mother, Eva, and her sister Irma. Enrique's aunt Rosa Amalia takes Jasmín back to Belky's hut, hoping to prevent a scene. Jasmín will have none of it. She's overheard some of the good-byes, and that Rosa Amalia is driving María Isabel to the bus terminal.

"I'm coming! I'm coming to drop off my mother," she tells Rosa Amalia, who finally allows her to come.

Jasmín runs to the car and gets in. María Isabel takes the backpack, which contains a change of clothes and one picture of her daughter. Belky climbs in, too, to see María Isabel off.

María Isabel gets out of the car and walks briskly into the bus terminal. She does not say good-bye to her daughter. She does not hug her. She does not look back. She tells herself that it is all right, that Jasmín doesn't really understand what is happening, where she is going, or for how long.

Rosa Amalia won't let Jasmín get out of the car. As the bus pulls out of the terminal, she tells the girl to say good-bye. Jasmín waves with both hands and calls out, *"Adiós, Mami. Adiós, Mami. Adiós, Mami. Adiós, Mami."*

10

UNEXPECTED REUNIONS

María Isabel travels up through Mexico on buses. With money from Enrique, smugglers sneak her through by bribing Mexican law enforcement officers. For part of the journey, the smugglers pack her and sixteen other migrants into the back of a truck, crammed together like sardines. María Isabel is nervous. She isn't certain she can trust her smuggler. But she is grateful to have him—it means she can avoid the trains Enrique had to ride atop.

One morning before dawn, as she is swimming across the Rio Grande into Texas, she loses her backpack in the river. In it is the only photograph she has brought of her daughter Jasmín.

Yet a few weeks after leaving Honduras, she arrives safely to join Enrique in Florida.

Back in Honduras, whenever four-year-old Jasmín hears the

drum of a plane engine overhead, she rushes outside. *"¡Adiós, Mami!"* she yells.

Jasmín, left with Enrique's sister Belky, asks, "Auntie, is my mommy coming back?"

"No," Belky answers, "your mommy is with your daddy."

Jasmín persists. "And she's not coming back?"

Belky tells Jasmín no, but that her parents will have her with them in the United States someday.

María Isabel misses waking up each day to bathe and dress Jasmín. She misses taking her on weekends to a doughnut shop for a treat. She misses their evening ritual, when the girl would drink a bottle of warm milk, rub her mother's belly, and slip into a deep sleep.

Enrique and María Isabel call their daughter every week from Florida. They ask Jasmín if she is behaving. Jasmín tells them everything she has done that week, the places she's been, how she plays with Belky's pet rabbits. She sings songs she learns in kindergarten. She tells them she wants to be with them in the United States.

Enrique talks of saving enough to buy a house and open a small store in Honduras someday. He talks of going back.

Lourdes is happy to be with Enrique, who is affectionate and well behaved. Yet she misses Belky terribly. She prays every night: God, give me my papers. I have my two youngest children with me now, and I want to finally be with my oldest. She says, "I ask God to give me this before I die." She sobs. "Is that so much to ask of God? I don't ask God for riches. Or other things."

On New Year's Day 2006, Lourdes calls Belky in Honduras. Belky is pregnant. She will give birth to Lourdes's second grandchild. Lourdes cries. "I fear I am never going to see you again," she tells her daughter. "I may see you only if I fulfill my dream of retiring in Honduras. You'll see me when I'm old."

On July 31, 2006, Belky gives birth to a baby boy, Alexander Jafeth.

❖ ❖ ❖

That summer, one of Spanish television's top-rated shows, *Don Francisco Presenta,* is taping a special episode on immigrant families that have been separated. Don Francisco has invited Enrique, Lourdes, and I to appear on the program. Don Francisco's show is widely watched in the United States and throughout Latin America. He is one of the most recognizable figures in the Hispanic world—a Latino combination of David Letterman and Oprah.

On September 11, 2006, Enrique, Lourdes, and I arrive to tape the show in front of a live audience. Before going on, Don Francisco asks Enrique about his past troubles with his mother. Enrique says things are much better now. They love each other very much. Enrique also tells Don Francisco that he works hard and focuses on saving money.

Don Francisco asks him if he still uses drugs. Enrique says he doesn't sniff glue—but does smoke marijuana when he goes out with friends. Don Francisco scowls with disapproval.

The show's audience cheers as Enrique, Lourdes, and I enter

through a white sliding door and sit next to Don Francisco on stage. Don Francisco fixes on one point: Are these separations, in the end, worth it? What do mothers and children who have experienced them think? Would they do it again?

Don Francisco asks Enrique, now twenty-three, how old he was when his mother left him. Five, Enrique answers.

"You were pretty mad at your mom?"

"Yes, I felt alone when I was in Honduras with my grandmother. My sister and I were separated. I felt resentful towards my mother for leaving us," he says.

Don Francisco turns to Lourdes. She is still torn about her decision to leave her children.

"Any mother feels bad when she leaves her children alone," Lourdes says. "But at the same time, it gave me strength and the courage to be here, knowing that he could have things he could never have had if I had stayed." Each month, she sent Enrique and his sister Belky money for food and for schooling. Her money has enabled Belky to graduate college and build a one-bedroom house in Honduras.

Don Francisco asks Enrique why he wanted to come to the United States.

"I wanted to get to know my mom. I only knew her through photographs."

At first, Enrique says, he was happy to see his mother. Yet with time, the resentment he felt toward her for leaving him came out. He rebelled against her.

Don Francisco asks Lourdes if it was worth it.

"To tell you the truth," Lourdes says, "on the one hand it

was worth it—at first. But on the other hand—no. I lost their childhood." She tells the talk show host she is glad to have two of her three children with her. "What I'm missing," Lourdes says, "is my other daughter." She hasn't seen Belky since she left her in Honduras in 1989.

Don Francisco's voice softens. "I know your biggest dream is to see your daughter after not seeing her for seventeen years."

Lourdes nods. Her voice tightens. She swallows hard, fighting back tears.

Don Francisco continues. "It's a frustration for you." Lourdes can't hold it in any longer. The mention of Belky makes emotion well up inside her. A tear rolls down each cheek. She quickly brushes the tears away. "I want you to think," Don Francisco says. "What would you want to say to your daughter, and what would you like to ask your daughter? I ask because today you are going to see her for the first time after seventeen years."

Lourdes's face becomes a river of tears. Her eyes go vacant. She is in shock.

Don Francisco asks, "You left her when she was . . . ?"

Lourdes sputters, "Seven years old."

Don Francisco turns to the white sliding door Lourdes and Enrique came through moments before. "Here is your daughter, Belky."

Lourdes stands. She looks around frantically.

Belky walks through the door and comes toward the stage.

When Lourdes glimpses Belky, her knees buckle. She forces herself to stay upright.

Arms outstretched, they meet and lock in an embrace. Lourdes shrieks with joy. "*Hija, te vinistes.* Daughter, you're here." Lourdes's and Belky's shoulders shake with each sob. They hold each other tight. Enrique stands. He embraces both of them—all three are together in a hug. He tells his sister she looks beautiful.

"I never expected this. I never expected this," Lourdes says, with tears of joy. "I love you so much. My daughter!"

Diana, Lourdes's American-born daughter, is in the audience. It is the first time Lourdes and her three children have been together in one room.

Don Francisco gives them a moment to calm down.

Belky tells him she has just given birth to a baby boy in Honduras. The boy is forty days old. It was hard to leave him in Honduras with her husband. She did so knowing this might be her only chance to get an American visa and come see her mother.

Don Francisco asks what she felt when hugging her mother after not seeing her for seventeen years.

Belky's voice fills with emotion. "Something unexplainable." She shakes her head, reaching for the right words. "After so long without her, it's very hard to explain what I feel. She knows I adore her. That I love her so much." Lourdes dabs at tears with a handkerchief.

Was the separation worth it? Belky says her mother has helped her a lot, and given her a life she never could have had otherwise. "But it never fills the emptiness I have felt for so long." Her hand taps her heart. "Not even now that I have my baby. The love of a mother is something you cannot replace with anything else."

Belky best answers Don Francisco's question eight days later. On September 19, 2006, she gets up early. At a Florida airport, she gives Lourdes one last tight hug. Then she boards an airplane back to Honduras.

Back to her son.

EPILOGUE

TWO PROMISES

When Enrique first arrives in the United States, he promises himself two things: to leave drugs behind and to bring his daughter north quickly.

Six months after María Isabel arrives in North Carolina, Enrique brings his four-year-old daughter, Jasmín, across the border and into the United States.

Jasmín journeys for ten days with Enrique's seventeen-year-old cousin and a woman the family trusts. The woman calls Enrique and María Isabel every day to reassure them. The girl travels through Mexico stashed away in the back of an eighteen-wheeler truck. She crosses the Rio Grande on an inflated inner tube, just like her father.

She is caught by Border Patrol agents as she is entering the United States but as a minor is quickly released to her parents with an order to appear in immigration court at a later date.

Jasmín runs toward her mother when she sees her.

"Mami!" she cries.

María Isabel sobs and embraces her daughter. But Jasmín, the girl with crooked teeth, curly hair, and a big smile, keeps her distance from Enrique. "He is your father," María Isabel insists.

Enrique tries to bridge the divide by spoiling his daughter. On weekends, when María Isabel is cleaning hotel rooms, Enrique takes Jasmín to the Golden Corral or McDonald's or to the mall to buy clothes. He watches *SpongeBob SquarePants* and *iCarly* with her. With each day, Jasmín grows closer to her father.

"You are my girl," Enrique says lovingly.

Like most parents in similar circumstances, Enrique and María Isabel are fearful of Jasmín being deported. The girl learns to hide behind cars on the street when she sees immigration agents.

In Florida, Jasmín becomes inseparable from her grandmother Lourdes. They spend so much time together people assume Jasmín is Lourdes's daughter. They dress alike, pull their dark curly hair up in high ponytails, wear dangly earrings. Lourdes heaps so much love and attention on the girl that Diana gets jealous.

"Everything I lost with Enrique I am enjoying with Jasmín—her childhood," Lourdes says.

A LAWLESS LAND

When Enrique moves his family to Florida, he rents in the same apartment complex as his mother, just one building over from her unit.

The gray, two-story apartments built of cinder blocks have large balconies in front of the second-floor apartments. On Friday and Saturday nights, many Latino men, their work-week done, gather on the balconies to sip beer and talk. Most are not in the United States legally, so they don't have bank accounts. They carry money from paychecks they received and cashed that day.

To a group of African American gangsters at the apartment complex, wads of cash, plus the fact that the Latino men are unwilling to report crimes to police for fear of being deported, make them an ideal target.

One Saturday evening in December 2006, Enrique and three friends are sipping Coronas outside after a week painting houses. Enrique moves to stand on the stairs leading up to his friend's balcony to take a call on his cell phone. Two attractive African American women brush past him and climb the stairs to the balcony. They flirt with his friends and ask to bum a cigarette.

Enrique's friends, distracted, don't notice a car with three African American men, parked out of sight around the corner, swing in front of their apartment.

The gangsters jump out of their car. They run up the stairs to the balcony.

Afraid his friend is about to be robbed, Enrique turns to follow the men up the stairs. One of the gangsters, brandishing a gun, grabs Enrique and flings him over the railing. Enrique crumples to the ground. He gets up and runs.

Two friends follow. Only one friend remains on the balcony.

The gangsters demand that he hand over his cell, a gold chain he is wearing, and his wallet, which contains just thirty dollars. They demand that he unlock his apartment door. Enrique's friend refuses.

The gangsters punch him in the stomach. They grab his throat. They slam the back of his head. Finally, one of the gangsters swings a twelve-gauge sawed-off shotgun at his face.

The blow splits open his forehead. He staggers, then falls to the ground. Conscious, he lies still as a stone, holding his breath, pretending he is dead, afraid the gangsters will finish him off. Blood streams from his head.

"He's dead," he hears one of the women say. The women and gangsters flee.

Sixteen stitches in his head save Enrique's friend. But the robbery is the beginning of constant fear for Enrique and his family.

For the next month, gangsters arrive at both Enrique's and his friends' apartment doors at two a.m. They knock loudly. "Police! Let us in!" Enrique peers out the peephole. It is not the police.

One day, as he is sitting outside on a bench near the apartment playground, someone shoots at Enrique. Another night, as he sleeps, someone rams into the front of his Toyota in the apartment parking lot, causing two thousand dollars' worth of damage. To Enrique and Lourdes it is intimidation, a clear message to not report what he witnessed in the beating to police.

"They didn't want witnesses," Lourdes said. "They wanted us to be afraid."

A month after Enrique's friend is beaten and robbed, the same gangsters beat and rob a Mexican man who lives in the apartment directly below Lourdes's. Drunk and enraged, the Mexican man runs into his apartment, grabs his machete, and chases the three gangsters. As he closes in on the gangsters, one of them turns around and shoots the Mexican man three times. The man, in his twenties, falls to the ground, dead.

In the spring of 2007, Lourdes's boyfriend finds that the three vans he uses for his house-painting business have been broken into. He loses thirteen thousand dollars' worth of tools, including two new sprayers and a compressor.

Latinos at the apartment complex start buying guns, fearful that gangsters might come into their apartments and kill their families. They stop sitting outside on benches by the playground, even during daylight. Lourdes's and Enrique's families don't go out at night, always keep their doors locked, and look through the peephole before opening the front door.

"It is like we are dogs locked up in a cage," Lourdes says. "We have so much fear."

Police step up patrols, and yet they never seem to be around when bad things happen, and as far as Enrique's family can tell, the beating of Enrique's friend, the murder of the Mexican, and the van break-ins all go unsolved.

Enrique never reports any crime against him to police. Like most immigrants in the United States illegally, he fears that calling the cops will lead to deportation. Worse, Lourdes fears that because she went on Don Francisco's television show without disguising herself and because many in the neighborhood have tied her to a bestselling book about un-documented immigrants, her family's odds of being deported are potentially higher.

Instead of turning to police, Enrique and Lourdes opt for a different solution. "The black people started killing the His-panics, so we decided to move," says Jasmín.

Lourdes vows she is done renting apartments. She rents a house.

LOCKED UP

In North Carolina, Enrique gave up glue sniffing. But in Flor-ida, he meets new friends who use different drugs.

In 2010, Lourdes convinces Enrique and his family to move back in with her. Her presence, she hopes, will help her son. Also, Enrique can help her cover her rent. Ever since the real estate bubble burst in 2007, hitting Florida particularly hard, Lourdes and her boyfriend have been struggling financially.

Lourdes's boyfriend has to let go his crew of twenty paint-ers. He begins working for an hourly rate. If there is no work locally, he goes to Georgia and Key West in search of jobs. Lourdes helps keep the family afloat with her job caring for two elderly Floridians.

In April 2010, Lourdes marries her longtime boyfriend, in keeping with the teachings of the church. Her daughter, Belky, follows in her footsteps, joining an evangelical church in Honduras and marrying her longtime boyfriend, Yovani, the same month.

For Lourdes, faith helps her manage disappointment in her children. "Since I came from Honduras, all I wanted was to have my children study, be well-raised," Lourdes says.

Belky never finishes college. She makes and sells fruit pops from the small home Lourdes built for her. Diana drops out of high school half a credit short of finishing. She talks of being a police officer but instead goes to work selling telephone plans for $9.50 an hour.

Enrique spends Christmas 2011 drinking with friends at a local motel, a run-down brick building with brown shutters and plywood patches on some of the doors.

At eight p.m. on December 26, sheriffs arrive at the motel. Enrique and four others are still in their motel room, drinking. Sheriffs discover that Enrique has an outstanding order of arrest for not paying a ticket he was issued three years ago for driving without a license. As part of the wave of local and state anti–illegal immigrant laws passed in recent years, only three states still allow undocumented immigrants to get driver's licenses.

Enrique spends the night in jail, expecting to be released.

When María Isabel, now three months pregnant, learns of his arrest, she cries hysterically.

In 2008, the federal government began rolling out a program every police department in the country had to implement by 2013: if someone is arrested for any reason, their fingerprints must be sent to federal immigration authorities, who will deport people who are in the United States illegally.

As the federal program was adopted by thousands of police departments, deportations increased 40 percent between fiscal years 2006 and 2011, a year when the United States deported nearly 400,000 immigrants nationwide. During those same five years, Florida nearly doubled the number of undocumented immigrants it had in its jails any given night.

The increased deportations put Enrique's family, and migrants around the country, in a state of constant fear. They have caused another kind of family separation: according to the think tank The Applied Research Center, the United States removed 46,000 parents of U.S. citizen children. At least 5,100 of those children ended up in foster care.

Jasmín, a girl who loves Justin Bieber, puppies, and dolphins and who dons a reflective vest to man her post every weekday as the student safety officer at her elementary school, is afraid every morning when her mother walks out the door to go to the grocery story or on an errand. "I worry," the girl says, "about my mom being deported."

The day after Enrique's arrest, sheriffs hand him over to immigration authorities, who place him in a county jail in Florida and begin deportation proceedings.

The county jail sets aside one of its two wings just for immigrant detainees. The county receives nearly $85 per day from the government to hold immigrants—an average of $21,264 per night in 2011.

The immigrant wing has eight locked areas, each with a high-ceilinged common area and two stories of cells along the perimeter. The inside of the jail is stark. The walls are cinder blocks painted eggshell. The floor is gray concrete. At night, immigrants are locked in their cells, which sleep two or four detainees.

Enrique tries to sleep atop the thin brown mattress on the narrow steel bunk bolted to the wall of his cell. The TV blares until midnight. Metal doors clang open and shut all night. Earplugs are prohibited. He cannot sleep. Purple rings circle his eyes.

County inmates are offered GED classes and AA meetings. Immigrants are not. The library cart arrives but Enrique sees only books in English, Russian, and French. Enrique understands everything the guards say and speaks passable English but cannot read it.

During the day, he is allowed out of his cell into a common area, which has four stainless-steel picnic tables and one TV. English- and Spanish-language migrants fight over what channel to tune in to.

Federal detention standards entitle immigration inmates to an hour of outdoor recreation. Jails lacking an outdoor area can substitute a large recreation room with free-flowing air and natural light. In Enrique's jail, the recreation room has one Ping-Pong table and two Wii screens for more than 240 inmates. Air and light come from one window at the top of the two-story room. The only time Enrique feels sunlight on his face is when he has a dental emergency. He can petition after six months to move to a jail with an outdoor area, but it would take him away from his family.

Instead, he paces, does push-ups, and plays chess because it takes a long time to finish a game. At night, he reads a Bible a prison chaplain gave him.

The only break from the monotony is when visitors arrive. Enrique cannot see them in person, or even through Plexiglas. He must view them on one of two video screens in the prisoners' common area right outside his cell.

A JOURNALIST'S DECISION

Lourdes looks for help. In January 2012 she calls me. Enrique is locked up, she says, and she must find a lawyer.

Journalists usually don't get involved personally with people they write about, because we must convey reality to readers, not write about a reality we have altered. Our credibility depends on playing it straight with readers, on not taking sides.

There is a clear exception to the no-involvement rule: if someone is in imminent danger, we should help them, if we can, and then we must disclose what we have done to readers.

I had followed how increasingly dangerous Honduras had become. The country now has the highest homicide rate in the world, according to the United Nations. Large swaths of Honduras, including Enrique's family's neighborhood, had fallen under the control of gangs and the Zetas, Mexico's most violent narco-trafficking organization.

The Zetas and other gangs impose an *impuesto de guerra*, a war tax, on drivers and business owners. At the taxi stand near Enrique's neighborhood, the Zetas' enforcer shows up every morning with a checklist of drivers. Anyone who hasn't paid the daily $13 tax is threatened or killed.

I learned that four of Enrique's close family members had been getting texts and telephone calls with death and extortion threats. The family changed phones and stopped going out at night.

The adult version of my book, published in 2006, had made Enrique famous in his neighborhood—and in Honduras. Three prominent TV shows about the book had been widely viewed in Honduras. When Belky went to the U.S. embassy to request a visa to visit the United States again, the official had cried, "You are the famous one! The one on TV!" To instill fear and earn greater notoriety, gangs in Honduras targeted and killed famous people. They had already murdered the previous president's son and a famous journalist. "If Enrique comes back, he is going to die," Belky told me.

I contacted several lawyers in Florida to help Enrique, now perhaps the most famous undocumented immigrant in America. His story had inspired changes in laws in Mexico and prompted readers to build schools and water systems and help establish businesses in Central America and in Mexico.

Two Miami attorneys, Sui Chung, at Immigration Law & Litigation Group, and Professor Michael S. Vastine, director of the Immigration Law Clinic at Saint Thomas University School of Law, stepped forward. They would pour many, many hours for free into Enrique's case and pursue two legal strategies: that either a past trauma or a future one he might face should save Enrique from deportation.

First, Enrique's attorneys laid the groundwork to apply for a U visa, a program created by Congress in 2000 that allows migrants to stay legally if they are victims of a crime, provided that they report that crime and then help prosecute the perpetrator by serving as witnesses. Congress envisioned the U visa as an invaluable tool to encourage migrants frightened of coming forward and cooperating with police because doing so could result in deportation or lethal retaliation from gangs.

Enrique's attorney Sui Chung believes the visa helps make many communities safer by giving migrants a powerful incentive to cooperate with authorities.

Enrique's attorneys offered local law enforcement authorities testimony in the beating Enrique had witnessed. Law enforcement certification of his cooperation with an investigation was critical for him to be able to apply for the visa.

Meanwhile, Congressional leaders had begun fighting about whether to curtail the visa program. The U.S. Senate approved increasing the number of U visas allowed annually to 15,000 from 10,000. They wanted to increase the incentive for frightened victims to come out of the shadows. But critics in the U.S. House of Representatives are incensed that this is the one visa where even aggravated felons aren't barred. What's more, they say, there is no numerical cap to the number of family members of victims who can get the visa. Granting a path to citizenship, they say, isn't proportional to helping police solve a crime. They are working to disallow the path to citizenship afforded by the visa.

There is no time limit for when a crime victim can step

forward to help police investigate a crime and thus be certified for a U visa for their efforts.

In the spring of 2012, local sheriffs reject Enrique's request. They do not consider Enrique's initial fear of approaching authorities because he believed he would be deported. They simply tell Enrique's attorneys that when the police report on his friend's beating was filed, Enrique wasn't listed as a witness. Enrique's attorneys focus on another claim that the U.S. government should allow Enrique to stay in the country because his notoriety would make him the target of the Zetas if he was deported.

A SON

On July 2, 2012, María Isabel goes into labor. Enrique, awaiting the outcome of his legal case, has been locked up for six months. He is in jail thirty-five miles away.

Daniel Enrique is born at 5:38 the next morning.

Enrique has now missed the birth of both of his children.

When he hears about his son's birth, Enrique momentarily considers signing papers to be deported to Honduras, despite the risk of being killed there. He feels frustrated hearing that friends and relatives who were deported are back in the United States in just one or two months.

Lourdes talks sense back into her son, urging him to think about all the time his attorneys have put into his case. She tells him he will be targeted and killed in Honduras.

She reminds him that the journey will be more dangerous than ever.

In 2011, prodded by human rights activists and accounts such as the adult version of *Enrique's Journey*, Mexico passes a law allowing Central Americans to travel legally through their country. A sign in Coatzacoalcos, Veracruz, actually welcomes Central Americans.

But the good done by that law is canceled out by the Zetas' seizing control of the central train route Enrique once took. People pretending to be smugglers turn migrants over to the narco-trafficking cartel. The Zetas beat and torture people to obtain information about relatives in the United States, and demand ransom from them.

In 2010, an eighteen-year-old relative of Enrique's set off for the United States and disappeared. In 2012, a sixteen-year-old who left from Enrique's neighborhood was kidnapped in Mexico. In a 2012 report, Human Rights Watch said that about 18,000 Central American migrants were being kidnapped each year crossing into Mexico. Those who don't have relatives with money are killed. Enrique's cousin who made the journey in 2012 estimates that a third of migrants get kidnapped.

If Enrique gets deported, returns to the United States, and again gets caught by police, the consequences could be severe. His attorneys have seen clients with no criminal history get eight years in jail for reentering the United States without permission.

Enrique, who still has a scar and a bump on his forehead from his journey in 2000, listens to his mother's arguments.

He stays put.

Enrique will ask the court for relief from deportation, which is granted to immigrants who fear persecution if they return home. Enrique acknowledges his troubled past but argues that everyone should have a chance at redemption. "We should all have a chance to change. I *am* changing my life," he says from jail. He wants to focus on his children, on María Isabel, on his mother, on himself. "I want to do something with my life."

Eleven days after the birth of his son, Enrique's immigration judge denies his claim to stay in the United States on all counts. He says Enrique is afraid to return to Honduras because gangs want to extort money from him, like they do everyone else. The judge says Enrique is in danger going back to Honduras but hasn't met a requirement of being allowed to stay in the United States: proving he is part of a persecuted group.

On July 19, 2012, the judge orders Enrique deported. Enrique watches the judge rule from a video camera at the county jail. It is one of the worst moments of his life.

The next month, his attorneys appeal.

SEPARATED BY A SCREEN

On September 23, 2012, a Sunday afternoon, Lourdes drives down a four-lane highway framed by towering pines to the county jail.

Each Sunday after church, she, Jasmín, and Daniel—and María Isabel, when she isn't working—visit Enrique.

She and Jasmín each grab one side of the baby carrier's handle. They lift Daniel and carry him between them.

They walk past a large American flag fluttering in the fall breeze and toward the one-story building with a green faux-stone façade.

Lourdes checks in and hands her ID to a guard at the visitation desk. He waves them over to video screen number 9, one of fifteen monitors, each in their own cinder-block visitation stall.

The small black video screen flickers on. Jasmín can see inside Enrique's jail unit. Soon, in an orange prison jumpsuit, Enrique approaches and sits before his screen.

Jasmín lifts a telephone receiver to talk. For nine months, ever since Enrique has been locked up, this is the only way she has been able to see her father.

When she first came, she was scared to go with Lourdes to the jail guard and sign in. Instead, she quietly sat in the corner of the visitation room, trying to catch a glimpse of Enrique on the far-off screen.

Today, she scoots her chair across the shiny linoleum floor, closer to the screen. She misses her father's hugs.

Lourdes stands next to Jasmín and holds Daniel, who has chubby cheeks and tufts of black hair and is dressed in a white onesie, up to the screen. "Look here! You are going to see your daddy!" Lourdes coos. Jasmín cradles the receiver to Daniel's ear.

"Say 'Hello, *Papi,*'" Jasmín tells her brother. Enrique smiles at his son, revealing two teeth still broken from his train ride. Lourdes tells Enrique his son is just as demanding as Enrique was as a baby. He always wakes up cranky, pouts his lips, puts his forearm across his eyes. Caring for this boy, so like what she remembers of Enrique as a baby, makes Lourdes smile.

Enrique looks at his son through the screen, emotion dancing in his eyes.

"I am your father. Behave yourself. Stop being difficult with your grandma!" His voice softens with love. Enrique waves at his screen. "How is my boy?"

His brown eyes transfixed, Daniel looks at Enrique. He drools and gurgles into the receiver.

Finally, Lourdes readies to leave, to be separated from Enrique for another week. "I love you a lot," she tells him.

Enrique braved eight attempts through Mexico to find his mother, but some Sundays these good-byes are more than he can endure. When he first saw Daniel, his arms ached to hold him.

Sometimes, he asks them not to visit. It is too hard not to hug Jasmín. He has never cradled or even touched his own son.

FAITH AND PRAYERS

Just before coming to the jail, Lourdes and Jasmín head to an evangelical church in a scrappy part of town. Inside the sunny stucco building is a cavernous room, painted in bright Caribbean colors. As the service begins, all of the hundreds of worshipers, who are immigrants from Colombia, Honduras, and Cuba, are out of their purple-cushioned chairs. They are on their feet, dancing and singing.

"I will rejoice in Jehovah!" Lourdes sings as she claps and

dances in her gold sequined open-toe platform shoes. "He has taken away all of my pain!" Jasmín, eleven, stands next to her, rocking her two-month-old brother in his bassinette.

For three hours, as she does every Sunday, Lourdes, clutching a large Bible, dances and sings and prays. She asks God to save her son from deportation, from death.

For if he is deported, the cycle will begin anew. Enrique will be separated not only from Jasmín, but also from his newborn son.

AFTERWORD

WOMEN, CHILDREN, AND THE IMMIGRATION DEBATE

An estimated one million children live illegally in the United States, most from Mexico and Central America. Like Enrique, almost all have spent time away from a parent before following him or her to the United States. Statistics show that one out of every four children in the nation's elementary schools is an immigrant or the child of an immigrant. This is nearly double the number in 1990.

Children leaving Central America to find their mothers in the United States today face a more hazardous journey than ever before. In the south of Mexico, in particular, they are likely to be kidnap victims.

To the north, in Nuevo Laredo, along the Rio Grande where Enrique camped, there are raging battles between drug dealers. The body of El Tiríndaro, the smuggler who crossed

Enrique into Texas, was found in February 2002 near the road to the Nuevo Laredo airport. He had been blindfolded, tortured, and shot in the head, execution-style. El Tiríndaro, whose full name was Diego Cruz Ponce, was one of fifty-seven murders in Nuevo Laredo that year, and the violence has gotten much worse since then.

The Zeta narco-trafficking organization seized control of Nuevo Laredo, and the city became a war zone. Shoot-outs in broad daylight became common. Bodies were hung from bridges, and the mayor's office was bombed. Local newspaper reporters stopped covering the drug violence after their offices were hit with a grenade launcher. In 2005, the new police chief, who vowed to bring law and order to the city, was gunned down hours after taking office.

Migrants were at the center of the growing violence. They were abducted in large groups from buses or the tops of trains. In 2010, on a Mexican highway leading to the Texas border, seventy-two migrants, most from Central America, were pulled off a bus and taken to a ranch by the Zetas, who became enraged and shot and killed the migrants one by one. Later that year, the bodies of 193 migrants were found in clandestine graves nearby. Police were led there by Zeta members who confessed to kidnapping and killing bus passengers, often migrants.

In December 2010, some fifty Central Americans were abducted after the train they were on was stopped and held up by gunmen in the southern state of Oaxaca. The same thing happened two years later to forty Central Americans in Veracruz.

Across the length of Mexico, there are more and more pregnant women and parents with young children who face riding the freight trains. Some parents carry babies in their arms.

Between 2001 and 2004, the number of Central American migrants detained and deported each year by Mexico nearly doubled, to more than 200,000. Most came from Guatemala, El Salvador, and Honduras and were trying to reach the United States. But as the recession cut jobs for migrants between 2005 and 2010, fewer headed north, and the number of Central American migrants caught in Mexico dropped by 72 percent. In 2012, as the U.S. economy brightened, the numbers apprehended in Mexico ticked up. In the summer of 2012, a friend of Enrique's got on a train in Chiapas loaded down with 1,500 other migrants.

The number of adults arriving unlawfully in the United States is at a forty-year low. But the number of children like Enrique coming alone has recently surged to record levels. In fiscal 2011, U.S. immigration authorities caught and detained some 14,000 children, mostly from Central America, double the previous year's figure. Another 16,000 Mexican unaccompanied minors were caught and immediately deported. Experts estimate that for every migrant who gets caught there are two or three who don't, which means an estimated 100,000 children came to the United States unaccompanied by a parent or other adult that year. These children are fleeing drug violence, forced recruitment into gangs, and poverty, and, like Enrique, they are searching for their mothers.

The U.S. government has sought to house this surge in

youngsters in fifty-three detention centers in twelve states; however, in 2012 these centers exceeded capacity. The federal government had to tap Lackland Air Force Base in San Antonio, Texas, and set up temporary tent facilities to house the overflow. They eventually added 900 beds to 2,800 that already existed in detention centers for children.

Since 2006—spurred by record numbers of unlawful immigrants and hostility fueled by a recession—there has been a wave of local and state laws passed aimed at addressing illegal immigration. These measures, meant to make life so miserable that immigrants will self-deport, prohibit migrants from renting apartments, getting driver's licenses, and securing jobs. Six states banned giving in-state tuition to students who are in the United States unlawfully; New Jersey and Florida tried to ban the lower tuition for U.S.-born children of undocumented immigrants as well. That move was rejected by state courts. States like Alabama denied illegal immigrant students any right to go to college, even if they were willing and able to pay higher out-of-state rates. (Twelve states passed laws allowing immigrant students in the United States unlawfully to pay in-state tuition.)

Between 2005 and 2010, nearly one thousand laws addressing illegal immigration passed state legislatures. Police find themselves having to act as de facto immigration agents, arresting and handing over unlawful migrants to federal immigration authorities. Six states, led by Arizona in 2010, passed sweeping legislation against illegal immigrants. The laws caused migrants to live in greater fear.

The issue remains as controversial as ever. The questions are still the same: Is immigration good for the migrants themselves? Is it good for the countries from which they are migrating? Is it good for the United States and its citizens?

EFFECT OF IMMIGRATION ON MIGRANTS

For immigrants, the practical benefits of coming to the United States are clear. The money Lourdes sent Enrique allowed him to eat, dress, and attend school longer. Once he arrived in the United States, Enrique drove his own truck and could make a decent living if he worked hard at his low-paying job. Enrique loves how clean the streets are compared to those in Honduras, how most people respect and obey the laws. Lourdes enjoys taking showers with indoor plumbing, as well as the relative safety of her neighborhood. She has the freedom to get in her car and go anywhere she wants.

Enrique acknowledges drawbacks that were clear to him before he was jailed. He must live in the shadows, knowing he can be deported at any time. He faces racism. When he goes into a restaurant and can't order well in English, he gets dirty stares. "They look at you as if you are a flea," he says. Salespeople in stores often attend to American customers first. Even Mexicans look down on Central Americans as inferior. Often employers pay immigrants less than they pay citizens—and assign them the most unpleasant tasks that no one else wants to do. Immigrants were harder hit by the recession and faced higher unemployment rates than American workers. A study by the Pew Research Center found that Hispanic household wealth dropped 66 percent during the recession, more than that of any other racial or ethnic group. Enrique scrambled sometimes to find work painting houses.

Life in the United States, Enrique and others say, is too hurried. In Honduras, people work half a day Saturday and rest Sunday. There is time to be with your family and enjoy a meal together. Here, Enrique paints seven days a week in an endless struggle to pay bills. "Here," he says, "life is a race."

Before 1990, immigrants went overwhelmingly to six states. But with the new influx of legal and illegal immigrants, 27 million in two decades, many migrants went to places that hadn't seen new immigrants in generations. Large numbers of Latino immigrants who spoke Spanish and had different customs arrived; the locals rejected rapid change and were hostile toward the newcomers. Legislators acted on that hostility, ushering in the biggest crackdown on unlawful immigrants in decades.

NEWCOMER TRAUMAS

For migrants, the biggest downside to coming to the United States is the damage caused by years apart for parents and children. That toll is most evident inside places like Los Angeles's Newcomer School, a transitional school for newly arrived immigrant students.

There, each day, the school's soft-spoken counselor, Gabriel Murillo, finds the small wooden box outside his office full of "request to see the counselor" slips. More than half of the 430 high school students will ask to see him by year's end. The reason? *Problemas familiares,* they write: family problems. Most have recently reunited with a parent, usually a mother. On average, they have not seen the parent in a decade.

Murillo sees some children who feel resentful even before coming north. Others have deeply buried anger that emerges after months with their mothers. They say their mothers lied to them from the start, promising to return quickly. They prayed that the Border Patrol would catch their mothers and send them back, arguing that they would rather be together, even if it meant going hungry. They demand that their mothers apologize for leaving them. They tell them that even a dog doesn't leave its litter.

Some children are angry because they had to leave behind the people who loved and nurtured them most—their grandmothers, who might now suffer a loss of their only source of income. What if they never see their grandparents again?

Mothers demand respect for their sacrifice, insisting that the separations were worth what was gained. They see their children as ungrateful brats. Beset by guilt, the mothers sometimes fail to discipline their children. These scars are often irreparable or take years to heal. Los Angeles Unified School District psychologist Bradley Pilon believes only one in ten immigrant students ultimately accepts his or her parent and puts the rancor behind them.

Often mothers lose what is most important: the love of their children.

Some mothers, Mr. Murillo says, do many things right. They leave children with relatives who constantly emphasize that the parents left to help their children. They keep in constant contact during the separation. They are open and honest about their lives in the United States. They never promise anything, especially a visit or reunion, until they are positive they can deliver. Even in these cases, Murillo says, the reunions are rocky. One mother says, "I think it's like the Bible says. People will move around. But not find peace."

Many reunified children, not finding the love they had hoped for with their mothers, search for love elsewhere, Mr. Murillo says. Some boys find a family in the local gangs and end up selling drugs. Some young women get pregnant and start new families of their own before they are ready. Gangs and pregnancy are much more common among reunited children than among those born here, says Zenaida Gabriel, a case manager at Sunrise Community Counseling Center, where some Newcomer School students go for help.

Newcomer School psychologist Laura Lopez estimates that only 70 of 430 students will complete high school. Indeed, immigration expert Jeffrey Passell says nearly half of all Central American children who arrive in the United States after the age of ten don't graduate from high school.

Special education teacher at Newcomer School Marga Rodriguez adds, "This isn't worth it. In the end, you lose your kids." But she admits she doesn't know what it's like not to have anything to feed your hungry children.

Oscar Escalada Hernández, director of the Casa YMCA shelter for immigrant children in Tijuana, Mexico, agrees: "The effect of immigration has been family disintegration. People are leaving behind the most important value: family unity."

The survivors, like Enrique, try to block out problems with their mothers and focus on what is good for them and their futures. They work to ensure that the love they feel for their mothers overcomes the rancor they also feel.

LANDS LEFT BEHIND

The departure of immigrants has been bittersweet for the countries they leave as well. Losing so much of the population has kept unemployment from climbing even higher: those who remain can have the jobs the migrants would have taken up otherwise.

Immigrants also send huge amounts of money from the United States to their families back home, typically one-tenth of what they make, which contributes more than $40 billion a year to the Latin American economy. It is used for food, clothing, and medical expenses, and to educate children. Grandparents who get money to care for children left behind would be destitute without the payments.

Immigrants who return to their home countries also bring back skills they learned from living in a country with more technology, says Norberto Girón of the International Organization for Migration in Honduras. Immigrants' desire to communicate with families back home in Honduras has resulted in improved telephone and Internet services. They also come back with stronger demands for democratic processes, says Honduran immigration expert Maureen Zamora.

But the separation of children and parents has lasting negative consequences in these Latin American countries.

Many of the 36,000 gangsters in Honduras come from families in which the mother has migrated north, says Zamora. Grandparents, guided by guilt that the child they are raising isn't with his mother, go light on discipline. They also worry that if the child complains and gets moved to another relative, the money the mother sends may go elsewhere as well.

A public advertising campaign launched in 2002 is one sign Honduras is facing damage caused by family separations. The advertisements run on television and radio, and are plastered on billboards at the Tegucigalpa bus station, where Hondurans head north. "Father, mother," reads an advertisement with a young girl on a swing. "Your children need you. Stay here. In Honduras there are opportunities to get ahead. Discover them!"

IMMIGRANT NATION

Each year, the United States legally admits nearly a million people, more than twice as many since the 1970s. Recession and greater border enforcement caused illegal immigration to drop by two-thirds since its peak in 2007, but three hundred thousand people still come to the United States unlawfully every year. Today, forty million residents of the United States were born in another country; nearly a third of those live in the United States illegally. Despite the recent slowdown, the decade between 2000 and 2010 had the highest number of immigrants coming to the United States ever recorded.

Today, while the proportion of people in the United States who are foreign-born is 13 percent—still slightly lower than the 15 percent peak reached in 1890—it has climbed from 5 percent in 1970. In California, more than one in four residents was born in another country.

Some Mexicans and Mexican Americans have jokingly dubbed the influx *la reconquista*—the reconquest of lands in the United States that were once held by Mexico.

Initially, Enrique and Lourdes disagree about the impact of this on the United States. Enrique says that were he an American citizen, he would want to restrict illegal immigration. Like most on his paint crew, he explains, he gets paid cash "under the table," which is to say he does not contribute taxes on what he earns. He uses publicly provided services, including emergency medical care. And he sends a portion of his income to Honduras, rather than spending it in his community.

Lourdes disagrees. Yes, she says, her daughter was born at a public hospital, and she received welfare for a time. Still, she pays taxes and is entitled to those services. To her, immigrant labor is the engine that helps drive the American economy. Immigrants like her, she says, work hard at jobs no American wants to do, at least not for minimum wage with no health benefits or paid vacation time. Immigrants' willingness to do certain backbreaking jobs at low wages provides goods and services to all Americans at reasonable prices, she says.

Over time, Enrique comes to think more like his mother on these issues. Immigrants, he says, clearly help the U.S. economy. He doesn't understand why police are targeting migrants.

Many Americans understand that being born in the United States, with all the opportunities that come with citizenship, is a matter of sheer luck. They are happy to share the opportunities that the United States provides with people who are desperate for a shot at a better life.

Others believe that U.S. policies with Latin America in the past have planted the seed for the current wave of immigrants. In recent decades, the United States has supported, and sometimes even helped install, repressive regimes in Latin America. These regimes fueled poverty, civil wars, and the resulting economic crisis that is now pushing so many Latin American citizens to migrate from their home countries to the United States. Today, demand in the United States for cocaine and marijuana has caused drug cartels and violence to boom south of the border.

Employers in the United States see other benefits. Being in the country illegally motivates people like Enrique to do good work and keep his employment stable. Enrique knows his family in Honduras depends on the money he sends. He works hard to keep his job. It would be tough to get another job because he is in the country illegally and doesn't speak fluent English.

Many experts say immigrants help the economy grow and prevent businesses that rely on cheap labor from being forced to close or ship jobs abroad. Immigrant women make up the majority of some low-education occupations, like cleaning, babysitting, or factory work. A 1997 study by the National Research Council that is considered among the most comprehensive assessments of the effects of immigration showed that immigrants lower the cost of nearly 5 percent of all goods and services everyone in America buys.

Immigrants' biggest contribution, others say, is how their presence brings new blood, new ideas, and new ways of looking at things that drive creativity and spur advances. A disproportionate number of the nation's high achievers, the NRC study noted, such as Nobel laureates, are immigrants from around the world. Indeed, it is often the most motivated people who are immigrants. Who else would leave everything they know, cross Mexico on top of freight trains, and come to a place where they have to start from scratch?

BENEFIT AND BURDEN

Some opposition to immigration is racism, a resistance to change, a discomfort with having people around who don't speak the same language or have similar customs. Yet some of the negative consequences of immigration are real, and are becoming increasingly evident as more women and children arrive.

Overall, the NRC said, immigrants use more government services than native-born Americans. They have more children, and therefore more kids in public schools. This is especially true for immigrants from Latin America, whose households are nearly twice as large as those of the native-born. It will cost the government two and a half times as much per household to educate their children, the study found.

Immigrants are poorer, have lower incomes, and qualify for more state and local services and assistance. Immigrant women receive publicly funded care during pregnancy. Their U.S.-born children are entitled to welfare, food stamps, and Medicaid. Compared to native households, immigrant families from Latin America are nearly three times as likely to receive government welfare payments for these children.

Because immigrants earn less money and are less likely to own property, they pay lower taxes. Some immigrants receive their salaries in cash and pay no income taxes at all.

The burden to taxpayers is greatest in immigrant-heavy states such as California, where an estimated half of all children have immigrant parents. There, nonimmigrant households pay more state and local taxes than the services they receive; conversely, immigrant households pay a lot less in taxes than the value of the government services they receive. The crush of immigrants has contributed to a decline of many public services, namely schools, hospitals, and state jails and prisons. Classrooms are overcrowded. Hospital emergency rooms have been forced to close, in part because so many poor, uninsured, nonpaying patients, including immigrants, are provided with free care. In Los Angeles County, jails have had to release prisoners early because of overcrowding caused, in part, by criminal immigrants. The Center for Immigration Studies, which seeks reduced immigration levels, found that in 2002, nationwide, households headed by illegal immigrants used $26.3 billion in government services and paid $16 billion in taxes.

Those hardest hit by the influx of immigrants are disadvantaged native-born minorities who don't have a high school degree—namely, African Americans and previous waves of Latino immigrants. They must compete for the same low-end jobs immigrants take.

Wages for high school dropouts, who make up one in fourteen native workers, have declined in recent years. Between 1980 and 2000, a Harvard University study found, the influx of immigrant workers to the United States cut wages for native workers with no high school diploma by 7.4 percent, or $1,800 on an average salary of $25,000.

Sometimes, whole industries switch from native to immigrant workers. In 1993, I looked at efforts to unionize Latino janitors in Los Angeles. Previously, the jobs had been largely held by African Americans, who had proudly succeeded in obtaining increased wages and health benefits. Cleaning companies busted their union, then brought in Latino immigrant workers at half the wages and no benefits. The employers benefited because they no longer had to treat their workers well. They are able to get away with this for the same reason that gangster violence and crime in Mexico toward Central Americans has gone underreported: if immigrants went to the police to complain, they would be found out as illegal and deported.

In 1996, I went to an ordinary block of two-bedroom homes in east Los Angeles to understand why nearly a third of California Latinos had supported Proposition 187, a voter initiative to bar illegal immigrants from schools, hospitals, and most public assistance. The measure passed and was later struck down by the courts.

For residents of the block, ill feelings toward illegal immigrants were grounded in how the newcomers had affected their neighborhood and their lives. For them, the influx had meant not cut-rate nannies and gardeners, but heightened job competition, lowered wages, overcrowded government services, and a reduced quality of life.

The newcomers who moved into the neighborhood were poor. Residents estimated that the block's population had tripled since 1970; up to seventeen immigrants were jammed into one small stucco house. Second- and third-generation Latinos on the block felt that their working-class neighborhoods bore the brunt of a wave of impoverished, unskilled workers. Immigrants were arriving at an unsettling pace, crowding people out of jobs as painters, mechanics, and construction workers, and lowering wages.

In the 1980s, the RAND Corporation, a Santa Monica think tank, found that the benefits of immigration outweighed the costs. By 1997, it was the opposite. They recommended the country slash legal immigration to 1970s levels.

Some immigration experts question whether it makes sense to allow so many immigrants with low levels of education from poor, underdeveloped countries when the United States needs to compete globally in industries requiring high levels of education, creativity, and know-how. Mexican immigrants arrive with an average of five to nine years of education.

Other experts focus on how adding more than a million immigrants a year to the United States' population affects overcrowding of parks, freeways, and the environment. With 311 million people, the United States has more than five times as many residents as when Ellis Island first welcomed new arrivals.

In Los Angeles County, the surge in immigrants helped cause the poverty rate to nearly double, to 25 percent, between 1980 and 1997. The effect, at least in the short term: a sea of poor and working-class neighborhoods amid islands of wealth.

SCHIZOPHRENIC POLICIES

In the end, any calculus of the benefits and burdens of immigration depends on who you are. People who own businesses and commercial interests that use cheap immigrant labor benefit the most from immigrants like Enrique and Lourdes. They get a ready supply of accommodating, low-cost workers. Other winners are people who hire immigrants for services: to care for their children and drive them to school, tend to their lawns, clean their houses, and wash their cars.

High school dropouts have the most to lose. So do residents of immigrant-heavy states such as California, where an estimated quarter of illegal immigrants live, because services immigrants use disproportionately, such as public schools, are funded with local and state taxes.

Polls show Americans in recent years have hardened their views of immigrants, particularly those who are in the country illegally. A growing proportion thinks the government should reduce immigration from current levels.

Many immigration observers believe U.S. officials have pursued a purposefully schizophrenic immigration policy. The government spends $11.9 billion a year on border enforcement and has five times as many border patrol agents along the nation's southwestern border as when the crackdown began in the 1990s. It has walled off nearly 700 miles of that divide. Politicians talk tough about catching illegal immigrants. Labor-intensive industries—agriculture, construction, food processing, restaurants, domestic help agencies—want cheap immigrant labor to bolster their bottom lines. Meanwhile, critics say, efforts to enforce many of the nation's immigration laws are weak.

Whenever immigration authorities make even passing attempts to enforce a 1986 law that allows employers to be fined up to $10,000 for each illegal immigrant they hire, businesses—onion farmers in Georgia, meatpacking firms in the Midwest—bitterly complain. President Obama has conducted "silent raids" of thousands of businesses such as Chipotle and American Apparel, requiring them to produce documents showing that employees' social security numbers and names match—or they must be fired. The government has imposed $100 million in fines, but employees say that without biometric markers, workers can simply provide employers the same name and social security number—and be fine. Similarly, a pilot project allowing some employers to check the immigration status of job applicants via telephone has never expanded nationally and remains voluntary on the federal level and in most states.

Recently, the legislative drive to enact anti-immigrant legislation has cooled, with 40 percent fewer bills introduced and 20 percent fewer bills passed by states in the first half of 2012. No Arizona-style bills have passed in 2012. In Georgia, where 2011's anti-immigrant legislation meant 40 percent of agricultural workers left the state, resulting in $140 million in crops rotting in the fields for lack of pickers, politicians are hearing from powerful business interests. In Arizona, five additional immigration bills proposed were soundly defeated, and the state senator and architect of the original immigration law was recalled.

Demographics are also causing lawmakers to reconsider, especially since Latinos, who are considered socially conservative and not necessarily a lock for the Democratic Party, will go from 17 percent to 30 percent of the population in 2050. Pushing anti-immigrant legislation might mean election defeat. In California, for instance, Proposition 187, a 1994 bill that denied unlawful immigrants access to all government services, including K–12 education, alienated Latinos from the state's Republican Party. Today, no Republican holds statewide office in California. In 2012, President Obama gained an election advantage by signing an executive order that allowed two-year relief from deportation for 1.7 million immigrants who came to the United States unlawfully as children.

For decades, politicians have put a lock on the front door while swinging the back door wide open. A crackdown on the U.S.-Mexico border, begun in 1993, was designed to shift immigrant traffic to more remote parts of the border, where Border Patrol agents have a tactical advantage. Since the buildup began, the numbers of agents patrolling the border and the amount of money spent on enforcement have both tripled, according to a 2002 study by the Public Policy Institute of California (PPIC). Yet there is no evidence, the PPIC concluded, that the strategy has worked. In fact, the number of immigrants in the United States illegally has grown more quickly since the border buildup began—at least until the recession made migrants realize they would be making the trip with no payoff.

More illegal immigrants now use smugglers (90 percent, compared to 70 percent before). Immigrants, particularly those from Mexico, once returned home after brief work stints in the United States. Today, the increasing difficulty and cost of crossing means more come and stay. The new strategy has also resulted in more than three hundred deaths each year, as migrants are forced to cross in areas that are less populated, more isolated, and more geographically hostile.

As long as the poverty such as Lourdes lived in exists, it is most likely that people will try to get to the United States, even if they must take enormous risks to get here.

There is a clear pattern in U.S. history: When we need

labor, we welcome migrants. When we are in recession, we want them to leave. During the Great Depression, the United States deported a million people of Mexican origin, including half who were in the country legally. During World War II, when labor was scarce, we started the massive Bracero guest worker program. In fiscal 2011, the U.S. Border Patrol saw a forty-year low in apprehensions of illegal immigrants—just 340,000, compared to 1.68 million in 2000. As the economy improves, will there be another influx, and the inevitable backlash?

In the United States, many immigration experts have concluded that the only effective strategy for change is to improve the economies of immigrant-sending countries, so people will not want or need to leave. Hondurans point out a few things that would help bring that about. They say the United States should promote more democratic governments that are willing to take on corruption and redistribute wealth. What if the Honduran government, like Mexico's, promoted family planning? In Mexico, that one campaign, reducing the number of children per family to 2.2 in 2012 from 6.8 in 1970, is perhaps the single most significant change affecting the need to migrate. If the United States gave a strong preference to trading goods from immigrant-sending countries, it would help spur growth in certain industries, such as textiles, that employ women in Honduras. Others believe the United States, a country that is known to be stingy with foreign aid compared with other industrial countries, should give more donations. Individuals, Hondurans note, can support nongovernmental organizations that encourage job-creating small businesses or improve the availability of education in Honduras, where 11 percent of children never attend school.

The same exodus of women and children is evident in so many parts of the world. There are 214 million migrants worldwide; 49 percent are women. In Europe alone, one hundred thousand unaccompanied children have arrived, typically from Afghanistan, Albania, and Northern Africa.

Most immigrants would rather stay in their home countries with their extended families. Who wants to leave home and everything he or she knows for something foreign, not knowing if he or she will ever return? Not many.

What would ensure that more women can stay home with their children, where they want to be? María Isabel's mother, Eva, says simply, "There would have to be jobs. Jobs that pay okay. That's all."

NOTES

The reporting for this book spanned five years. During that time, I spent a total of six months, in 2000 and in 2003, in Honduras, Guatemala, Mexico, and North Carolina. The initial travel was done for a newspaper series for the *Los Angeles Times*. Subsequent travel and interviews would expand the series into this book. I found Enrique in Nuevo Laredo, Mexico, in May 2000, before he reached his mother. I spent two weeks with him there and rejoined him at the end of his journey in North Carolina, where he had reunited with his mother. Then, based on extensive interviews with him in Mexico and during three visits to North Carolina, I retraced each step he had taken, beginning at his home in Honduras.

Between May and September 2000, I spent three months working my way north through Mexico just as Enrique had, riding the tops of seven freight trains and interviewing people Enrique had encountered, along with dozens of other children and adults making the same journey. I walked around immigration checkpoints and hitchhiked with truckers, exactly as Enrique had. To retrace Enrique's steps, I traversed thirteen of Mexico's thirty-one states.

Though I witnessed a part of Enrique's journey, much of his

travel and life come from the recollections of Enrique and his mother. Enrique recalled his travel experiences largely within weeks of when they occurred. The recalled scenes and conversations were corroborated, whenever possible, by one or more individuals present. I conducted hundreds of interviews in the United States, Honduras, Mexico, and Guatemala with immigrants, immigrant rights advocates, shelter workers, academics, medical workers, government officials, police officers, and priests and nuns who minister to migrants. At four INS detention centers in California and Texas and in two shelters for child migrants in Tijuana and Mexicali, Mexico, I interviewed youngsters who had made their way north on top of freight trains. I conducted interviews from Los Angeles and also consulted academic studies and books about immigration.

In 2003, I retraced Enrique's journey for a second time. I spent time in Honduras with Enrique's family; his girlfriend, María Isabel; and their daughter, Jasmín. I witnessed some of the scenes depicted of María Isabel's life with her daughter. I again traveled through Honduras and Guatemala and retraced the rail route, starting in Tapachula, Chiapas, Mexico. To obtain additional details on the journey and people who help migrants along the rails, I spent time in five regions of Mexico.

I spent two weeks with Olga Sánchez Martínez, a shelter worker in Tapachula, Mexico, and a week with Father Leonardo López Guajardo at the Parroquia de San Jose in Nuevo Laredo, Mexico. I made a fourth trip to North Carolina to interview Enrique, Lourdes, and others in their family. In 2004, during a visit by Lourdes to Long Beach, California, I accompanied her to places where she once lived and worked. Between 2000 and the present, I have kept up with the family by visiting them both in 2011 and 2012, and have conducted regular interviews with Enrique, Lourdes, and several members of their family in Honduras by telephone.

The decision to use only the first names of Enrique and Lourdes is a continuation of a decision made by the *Los Angeles Times* that I support. The newspaper has a strong preference for naming the subjects of its articles in full. It did so with two members of Enrique's family and a friend. But the *Times* decided to identify Enrique and his mother, father, and two sisters by publishing only their first names and to withhold the maternal or paternal name, or both, of six relatives, as well as some details of Enrique's employment. A database review by *Times* researcher Nona Yates showed that publishing their full names would make Enrique readily identifiable to authorities. In 1998, the Raleigh, North Carolina, *News and Observer* profiled an illegal immigrant whom it fully identified by name and workplace. Authorities arrested the subject of the profile, four of the person's coworkers, and a customer for being undocumented immigrants. The *Times*'s decision was intended to allow Enrique and his family to live their lives as they would have had they not provided information for this story. For the same reason, I have decided in this book to identify Enrique's girlfriend by her first name and to withhold the maternal or paternal name, or both, of her relatives.

The following is an accounting of where information in this book comes from. It is an extensive but by no means complete list of the people who helped make it possible for me to tell Enrique's story. Throughout the book, people's ages and titles are for the time when Enrique made his journey. Despite the precautions taken while writing *Enrique's Journey*, following his detention by immigrant authorities in December 2011, immigration officials have now linked him to the book.

PROLOGUE

Information about the number of legal and illegal immigrants comes from the U.S. Department of Homeland Security's Office of Immigration Statistics and demographer Jeffrey S. Passel, a senior research associate at the Pew Hispanic Center. Passel estimated that since 2000, an average of one million illegal immigrants arrive each year.

The estimate that at least 48,000 children enter the United States from Central America and Mexico each year, illegally and without either parent, comes from 2001. It was reached by adding the following numbers: The U.S. Immigration and Naturalization Service (INS) said it had detained 2,401 Central American children. The INS had no figure for Mexican children, but Mexico's Ministry of Foreign Affairs said the INS had detained 12,019 of them. Scholars, including Robert Bach, former INS executive associate commissioner for policy, planning, and programs, estimated that about 33,600 children are not caught. For 2000, the total was 59,000.

Information about the initial wave of immigrants who were single mothers and came to the United States is from Pierrette Hondagneu-Sotelo, a sociology professor at the University of Southern California, and Wayne Cornelius, director of the Center for Comparative Immigration Studies at the University of California, San Diego. Hondagneu-Sotelo also provided numbers for the estimated growth in U.S. domestic worker jobs in the 1980s.

The University of Southern California study that discusses how many live-in nannies have left children behind is "I'm Here but I'm There: The Meanings of Latina Transnational Motherhood," published in 1997. The Harvard University study that details the percentage of immigrant children separated from a parent during the process of immigration is "Children of Immigration," published in 2001.

The description of how migrants arrived in Nuevo Laredo after having lost the phone numbers they were carrying comes from Deacon Esteban Ramírez Rodríguez of the Parroquia de Guadalupe in Reynosa, Mexico, and several migrant children stranded in Nuevo Laredo, including Ermis Galeano and Kelvin Maradiaga. Migrant twins José Enrique Oliva Rosa and José Luis Oliva Rosa told of having been kidnapped.

1. THE BOY LEFT BEHIND

Much of the account of Enrique's and Lourdes's lives in Honduras, Lourdes's departure from Honduras, their lives apart, and Enrique's departure to find his mother are drawn from Enrique, Lourdes, and family members. These include Enrique's sister, Belky; his aunts Mirian, Rosa Amalia, and Ana Lucía; his uncle Carlos Orlando Turcios Ramos; his maternal grandmother, Águeda Amalia Valladares, and paternal grandmother, María Marcos; his mother's cousin María Edelmira Sánchez Mejía; his father, Luis, and stepmother, Suyapa Álvarez; his girlfriend, María Isabel, and her aunt Gloria; Enrique's cousins Tania Ninoska Turcios and Karla Roxana Turcios; and Enrique's friend and fellow drug user José del Carmen Bustamante.

Lourdes elaborated on her description of being abandoned in 1989 at a downtown Los Angeles bus station by her smuggler by returning to the station with me in 2004. During the 2004 trip, further details of Lourdes's life in Long Beach were obtained as Lourdes took me to places where she had once lived and worked, including a Long Beach bar. Several of Lourdes's Long Beach friends were also interviewed and corroborated how they and Lourdes had been scammed by a woman claiming she could help them become legal residents.

For the account of Enrique's life with his paternal grandmother,

I visited the home of the grandmother and the home of Enrique's father, as well as the market where Enrique sold spices.

Santos's return to Honduras comes from Lourdes and her family members in Honduras, who said they had witnessed his behavior. Santos himself couldn't be located.

The smugglers' fees for bringing Central American children to the United States come from immigrant women and Robert Foss, legal director of the Central American Resource Center in Los Angeles.

2. REBELLION

Accounts of Lourdes's life in North Carolina come from Lourdes, her boyfriend, her daughter Diana, and their friends and relatives.

The description of the Tegucigalpa dump and its scavengers comes from my observations and interviews with children at the dump. I also witnessed children hauling sawdust and firewood. I spent time at the school in El Infiernito, where children arrive without shoes.

The description of María Isabel's childhood, her move to her aunt Gloria's house, and her devotion to Enrique is from Gloria, María Isabel, her sister Rosario, her brother Miguel, and her mother, Eva, and from time I spent at Gloria's and Eva's homes in Tegucigalpa.

The account of life in El Infiernito is from my visit to the neighborhood accompanied by the teacher Jenery Adialinda Castillo. I accompanied the Tegucigalpa priest Eduardo Martín on his evening rounds to feed glue-sniffing homeless children.

Enrique's attempt to reach his mother in 1999 was corroborated by José del Carmen Bustamante, his companion on the journey.

3. SEEKING MERCY

The descriptions of Enrique's first six attempts to reach the United States are based on interviews with Enrique and my observations of other migrants along the same route. I visited the spot near Medias Aguas where Enrique was stung by bees. I went to the Tapachula cemetery and the mausoleum where Enrique slept.

Stories of Enrique's experiences in and around Las Anonas were written from interviews with Sirenio Gómez Fuentes; Mayor Carlos Carrasco; Carrasco's mother, Lesbia Sibaja; residents Beatriz Carrasco Gómez, Gloria Luis, and other villagers; San Pedro Tapanatepec mayor Adan Díaz Ruiz; and the mayor's driver, Ricardo Díaz Aguilar. I visited the Fuentes home, the Las Anonas church, and the mango tree where Enrique collapsed.

Mayor Díaz provided the doctor's receipt detailing Enrique's treatment. The details of Enrique's medical condition and treatment come from Enrique and Dr. Guillermo Toledo Montes, who treated him.

The account of the bus ride to Guatemala is based on interviews with Enrique, migrants on the bus, and my observations while riding the bus to El Carmen, Guatemala, where the trip ends.

4. FACING THE BEAST

The story of the crossing of the Río Suchiate is based on interviews with Enrique, other migrants who made the crossing, and my observations as I crossed on a raft. The story of facing Chiapas, "the beast," is from Father Flor María Rigoni. The lessons about Chiapas come from Enrique, other migrants, and Father Arturo Francisco Herrera González, a Catholic priest who helps migrants at the Parroquia de San Vicente Ferrer in Juchitán, Oaxaca.

The story of how Enrique slept in the Tapachula cemetery and ran for the train comes from interviews with Enrique and from my observations at the cemetery of the ritual of running for the train. I accompanied the Tapachula municipal police on a dawn raid of the cemetery, did a tour of the cemetery with its caretaker, and visited the crypt where Enrique slept. To describe Enrique's trip to a Tapachula jail, I accompanied migrants who were captured by police and taken to the same lockup. The train's speed is from Jorge Reinoso, who in 2000 was chief of operations for the Ferrocarriles Chiapas-Mayab railroad, and from Julio César Cancino Gálvez, an officer of Grupo Beta, who is a former Tapachula train crewman. "The train ate him up" comes from Emilio Canteros Mendez, an engineer for Ferrocarriles Chiapas-Mayab, and was confirmed by migrants I met on the trains. The dangers of Chiapas were explained by Father Rigoni.

The strategies for preventing rape were detailed by Grupo Beta officers and Monica Oropeza, executive director of Albergue Juvenil del Desierto, a migrant shelter for minors in Mexicali, Mexico. The 1997 University of Houston study "Potentially Traumatic Events Among Unaccompanied Migrant Children from Central America" details the dangers minors encounter. The AIDS warning that girls write on their chests is from Olivia Ruiz, a cultural anthropologist at the Colegio de la Frontera Norte in Tijuana, who researches the dangers migrants face riding trains through Chiapas.

The description of how a train feels and choosing where to ride and what to carry comes from Enrique and from my observations and interviews with migrants while riding on two freight trains through Chiapas. Reinoso provided information about the age and condition of tracks in Chiapas and the frequency of derailments, one of which I witnessed. Train nicknames are from migrants, Grupo Beta officers, and former crewman Julio César Cancino Gálvez.

Tales of avoiding branches and what migrants yell when they see a branch come from Enrique and from my observations on the top of a train when a migrant was knocked off.

The dangers of La Arrocera were detailed by Enrique, other migrants, Grupo Beta officers, and the immigration agent Marco Tulio Carballo Cabrera at the nearby Hueyate immigration station. I observed migrants' anxiety as they approached the checkpoint on two train rides through La Arrocera.

The assertion that agents shoot at migrants at the La Arrocera checkpoint comes from C. Faustino Chacón Cruz Cabrera; Hugo Ángeles Cruz, an immigration expert at the Colegio de la Frontera Sur in Tapachula, Mexico; railroad employees who said they had witnessed such shootings, including José Agustín Tamayo Chamorro, chief of operations at Ferrosur railroad, and Emilio Canteros Mendez; and migrants who said agents had fired at them at La Arrocera, including Selvin Terraza Chan, age twenty-one; José Alberto Ruiz Méndez, age fifteen; and Juan Joel de Jesús Villareal, age fifteen. Hernán Bonilla, age twenty-seven, showed Enrique and me scars he said came from cigarette burns received from immigration agents in the area.

The description of bandits and their activities at La Arrocera comes from Julio César Cancino Gálvez, who again accompanied me to the checkpoint in 2003. I obtained additional information about bandits then from local *migra* supervisor Widmar Borrallas López and La Arrocera rail side residents Amelia López Gamboa, Jorge Alberto Hernández, Virgilio Mendes Ramírez, María del Carmen Torres García, and three men who feared giving their names. I also took a tour of the bandits' favorite bars in the nearby town of Huixtla.

Stories of how migrants hide their money come from migrants I met riding on the trains. The account of Enrique's run around La Arrocera comes from Enrique himself; Clemente Delporte Gómez, a former Grupo Beta Sur officer; and my observations as I walked around the checkpoint, witnessed two bandit chases, and entered the brick house where women had been raped.

The Cuil bridge ambushes were described by Clemente Delporte Gómez and Grupo Beta Sur officer José Alfredo Ruiz Chamec.

Accounts of the dislike of Central American migrants come from migrants, professor Hugo Ángeles Cruz, and Tapachula residents, including Miguel Ángel Pérez Hernández, Guillermina Gálvez López, and Juan Pérez. While riding trains through Chiapas, I witnessed Mexican children pelting migrants with rocks.

The account of María Isabel's reaction to Enrique's departure comes from María Isabel; her aunt Gloria; and her mother, Eva. The account of María Isabel's foiled plan to follow Enrique to the United States comes from María Isabel; her mother, Eva; her aunt Gloria; and Gloria's daughter Gloria Elizabeth Chávez.

The account of heat on the train and how migrants stayed awake is from Enrique. I witnessed migrants doing similar things to stay cool and awake, including Reynaldo Matamorros, who strapped himself to the end of a hopper car to nap; José Rodas Orellana, who took amphetamines; and José Donald Morales Enriques, who did squats. I rode on one train where a chorus broke out at four a.m.

Details about how gangsters stalk migrants come from Grupo Beta officers, Baltasar Soriano Peraza, and my observations on the trains. The account of how street gangsters rob riders is from Baltasar Soriano Peraza, the caseworker at the Albergue Belén shelter; the Mexican immigration agent Fernando Armento Juan, who accompanies migrants on the bus; and migrants, including Carlos Sandoval, a Salvadoran, who says he was accosted by gangsters with ice picks.

For accounts of how migrants are devoured by the train, in 2000,

I interviewed Carlos Roberto Díaz Osorto in his hospital bed in Arriaga, Chiapas. I later viewed his medical file.

In 2003, I spent two weeks with Olga Sánchez Martínez. I spent time with her at her shelter as she dressed migrants' wounds and accompanied her to church, to a prosthesis maker, to sell used clothing, on rounds at the local hospital, on a beach outing with injured migrants, and in her efforts in the middle of the night to find a casket for someone who had just died at her shelter.

To write about Olga, I spoke with migrants living at her Shelter of Jesus the Good Shepherd, including Tránsito Encarnación Martínes Hernández, Fausto Mejillas Guerrero, Leti Isabela Mejía Yanes, Hugo Tambrís Sióp, Edwin Bertotty Baquerano, Juan Carlos Hernández, Francisco Beltrán Domínguez, Efren Morales Ramírez, Carlos López, Fredy Antonio Ávila, and Mario Castro. I interviewed Olga; her husband, Jordán Matus Vásquez; her friends; and shelter volunteers Marilú Hernández Hernández, Fernando Hernández López, Roldán Mendoza García, and Carmen Aguilar de Mendoza.

5. GIFTS AND FAITH

The description of the statue of Christ comes from interviews with Enrique and from my observation of other migrants on a train passing the same statue. Information about religious items, Bible readings, and how migrants show their faith is from migrants Marco Antonio Euseda, Oscar Alfredo Molina, and César Gutiérrez. I heard migrant Marlon Sosa Cortez recite the prayer to the Holy Trinity as he rode on top of a train.

The account of the exchange between food throwers and Enrique comes from Enrique and is similar to words I heard while observing food throwers in various towns and as food throwers in Encinar, Veracruz, threw bananas and crackers onto a train I was riding. In Veracruz, I interviewed food throwers in several villages. At Encinar: Ángela Andrade Cruz; Jesús González Román, his sister Magdalena González Román, and their mother, Esperanza Román González; Mariano Cortés; and Marta Santiago Flores and her son Leovardo. At Fortín de las Flores: Ciro González Ramos, his children Erika and Fabián, and a former neighbor, Leticia Rebolledo. At Cuichapa: Soledad Vásquez and her mother, María Luisa Mora Martín. At Presidio: Ramiro López Contreras and his son Rubén López Juárez.

The assertion that Oaxacans are friendlier is based on interviews with Enrique and other migrants, as well as with Jorge Zarif Zetuna Curioca, the former mayor of Ixtepec; Juan Ruiz, the former police chief of Ixtepec; and train engineer Isaías Palacios.

For the account of the decision to help migrants at the Parroquia María Auxiliadora in Río Blanco, Veracruz, I relied on the priest Salamón Lemus Lemus; the volunteers Luis Hernández Osorio, Gregoria Sánchez Romero, and Leopoldo Francisco Maldonad Gutiérrez; the church cook, Rosa Tlehuactle Anastacio; the church secretary, Irene Rodríguez Rivera; Father Julio César Trujillo Velásquez, the director of media affairs for the Diocese of Orizaba; and Monsignor Hipólito Reyes Larios, the Catholic bishop of Orizaba.

In 2003, I interviewed various Veracruz church members who helped migrants with food, shelter, or protection from the police, including Raquel Flores Lamora, Baltasar Bréniz Ávila, Francisca Aguirre Juárez, and María del Carmen Ortega García.

The account of the beating of migrants in El Campesino El Mirador comes from María Enriqueta Reyes Márquez, who witnessed the incident, and Samuel Ramírez del Carmen of the Mendoza, Veracruz, Red Cross.

The story of Enrique's robbery at the Córdoba station comes from

Enrique and from my observations at the shed where it happened. Other migrants gave accounts of similar robberies at Córdoba.

Manuel de Jesús Molina, who in 2000 served as assistant to the mayor of Ixtepec, a nearby town, said that Enrique's experience of being robbed by the judicial police was common in the area. The denial that judicial police rob people comes from Sixto Juárez, chief of the Agencia Federal de Investigación in Arriaga, Mexico.

The tales of camaraderie with others aboard the train north of Orizaba and preparations for the cold are from Enrique and from my observations of other migrants at Orizaba. The description of tunnels is from Enrique and the switchman Juan Carlos Salcedo, and from observations by *Los Angeles Times* photographer Don Bartletti and me as we rode through the tunnels on top of a freight train.

Information on the danger of the El Mexicano tunnel is from José Agustín Tamayo Chamorro of the Ferrosur railroad. Accounts of what migrants yell as they ride through the tunnels and what they do to keep warm come from Enrique and were confirmed by my observations.

In 2000, I found the Mexico City culvert where Enrique waited for a train.

The reluctance to help Central Americans was described by Raymundo Ramos Vásquez, director of Comité de Derechos Humanos, Grupo 5 de Febrero, a human rights group in Nuevo Laredo, and Marco Antonio Valdez, a resident. The statement that Jesus was a migrant comes from Oscar Alvarado, caretaker for the Parroquia de San José's migrant shelter, and was confirmed by Enrique and other migrants.

In 2003, I returned to interview Lechería residents Olivia Rodríguez Morales and Oscar Aereola Peregrino and Lechería station personnel director José Patricio Sánchez Arrellano, who gave me a tour and history of the station. The account of the electrical lines in Mexico City is from Enrique and Cuauhtemoc González Flores of Transportación Ferroviaria Mexicana and from my observations at the railroad's computer center.

The number of security officers at the San Luis Potosí station is from Marcelo Rodríguez, chief of security at the station for Transportación Ferroviaria Mexicana.

The account of Enrique's stay in San Luis Potosí making bricks comes from Enrique and interviews with brick makers, including Gregorio Ramos, José Morales Portillo, and Juan Pérez. The account of Enrique's trip to Matehuala comes from Enrique and from my observations during a bus ride on the same route.

The reluctance of truck drivers to give migrants a ride was confirmed by Modesto Reyes Santiago, a truck driver, and Faustina Olivares, owner of the No Que No diner, which is frequented by truckers. I also hitchhiked on a truck between Matehuala and Nuevo Laredo.

6. ON THE BORDER

The description of the encampment is from Enrique and camp residents Hernán Bonilla, Miguel Olivas, Luis Moreno Guzmán, and Jorge Enrique Morales, as well as from my observations at the camp.

The portrayal of El Tiríndaro, his heroin habit, and his protection of Enrique is from my observations and interviews with Enrique and the camp residents Miguel Olivas, Hernán Bonilla, and Omar Martínez Torres. In 2003, I interviewed one of El Tiríndaro's Los Osos associates, Juan Barajas Soto, when he was in the Nuevo Laredo jail, Centro de Readaptación Social No. 1, who provided additional details about El Tiríndaro, Los Osos, and Enrique's stay at the encampment. The migrant Jorge Enrique Morales gave Enrique bits of tacos and contributed to the picture of life at the camp.

I observed Enrique washing cars for money.

The account of meal cards comes from Father Filiberto Luviano Mendoza at the Parroquia del Santo Niño and volunteer Leti Limón at the Parroquia de San José. Migrant Miguel Olivas described the meal-card black market.

The account of Father Leonardo López Guajardo's assistance to migrants comes from an interview with the priest in 2000 and with Sisters Elizabeth Rangel and María del Tepeyac. In 2003, I spent a week with the priest. I followed him to church; as he said Mass in a cemetery and to incarcerated prisoners; and as he traveled throughout Laredo, Texas, and Nuevo Laredo, Mexico, to pick up donated food, clothing, and other items. I interviewed people who donated goods to the priest, including Sister Isidra Valdez, Lydia Garza, Rosalinda Zapata, Margarita Vargas, and Eduardo Brizuela Amor. I spent time with two nuns helping him, Sisters Leonor Palacios and Juanita Montecillo.

To better understand the priest and his work with migrants, I spoke with the church secretaries Alma Delia Jiménez Rentería and María Elena Pineda de Aguilar, and the church volunteers Patricia Alemán Peña, Miguel Delgadillo Esparza, Pedro and Leti Leyva, José Guadalupe Ramírez, Horacio Gómez Luna, Rogelio Santos Aguilar, Rocío Galván García, Juana R. Cancino Gómez, and Felipa Luna Moreno. I interviewed Carlos Martín Ramírez, a doctor who treats migrants pro bono for the priest. I spoke with the church's neighbors Juana Mexicano de Acosta and Juan Acosta Hernández.

Father Leonardo López Guajardo at the Parroquia de San José calculated the percentage of the church's meals that go to children. I observed dinner for migrants at the Parroquia de San José and how migrants gathered around the map of Texas after the meal to discuss their route.

I interviewed and observed the lives of other children Enrique met in Nuevo Laredo who were also going to find their mothers, including Ermis Galeano, Mery Gabriela Posas Izaguirre, her aunt Lourdes, and Kelvin Maradiaga.

Talk of hardships and injuries during the trip north by migrants outside the Parroquia de San José comes from my observations of these conversations and from María del Tepeyac, a nun who ran the church's medical clinic.

The account of Enrique sleeping in the abandoned house, which I visited, comes from Enrique and photographer Don Bartletti's observations.

The rendering of Mother's Day comes from Central American mothers, including Águeda Navarro, Belinda Cáceres, Orbelina Sánchez, and Lourdes Izaguirre, and from my observations as they consoled one another. A mother's prayer to live is from my observations as I watched Lourdes Izaguirre pray.

Accounts of Lourdes's thoughts and actions after her son left home are from Lourdes and were confirmed by her cousin María Edelmira Sánchez Mejía, with whom Lourdes spoke at the time.

Accounts of Enrique's glue-sniffing habits are from Hernán Bonilla and from my observations. Juan Barajas Soto, who was interviewed at the jail in Nuevo Laredo in 2003, recalled Enrique's hallucinogenic talks with trees at the camp and his discussions about wanting to be with his mother.

I saw Enrique shortly after he got his tattoo and watched as he struggled to obtain his second phone card. The story of Enrique's effort to beg for money in downtown Nuevo Laredo comes from Enrique and Hernán Bonilla.

Accounts of the dangers of the river and checkpoints come from the migrants Miguel Olivas, Hernán Bonilla, and Fredy Ramírez; the U.S. Border Patrol supervisor Alexander D. Hernandez and officers Charles Grout and Manuel Sauceda in Cotulla, Texas; and my observations.

The description of the desert dangers is based on interviews with the migrants Miguel Olivas, Gonzalo Rodríguez Toledo, Luis Moreno Guzmán, Elsa Galarza, Leonicio Alejandro Hernández, Mario Alberto Hernández, and Manuel Gallegos; U.S. Border Patrol agents Charles Grout and Manuel Sauceda and the dog handler Ramón López; and my observations while accompanying agents for three days on the Texas border.

The General Accounting Office says at least 367 migrants died crossing the southwestern border into the United States in 2000.

7. DARK RIVER CROSSING

The story of Enrique's one a.m. departure is drawn from interviews with Enrique and migrant Hernán Bonilla, who witnessed the departure, as well as my subsequent observation of the staging area on the south bank of the Rio Grande and my observation of other nighttime crossings and pursuits by the U.S. Border Patrol. El Tiríndaro's words to Enrique and the two Mexicans about getting caught are from Enrique. Other migrants told me that this is a standard speech from smugglers to migrants before they cross the river.

The story of the drowning in the river is from Enrique and other migrants, including three at the Parroquia de San José. The migrants said they had watched a youngster named Ricki drown in a whirlpool two nights before.

The account of crossing to the island and then to the United States is from interviews with Enrique and from my subsequent observation of the island from Enrique's crossing site on the south bank of the river. I retraced Enrique's steps on both sides of the river and went to the spot where he had first touched U.S. soil.

A description of the jails where migrant children are held when they are caught by U.S. authorities comes from time I spent in these facilities, including a week at Los Angeles's Los Padrinos Juvenile Detention Center and a week in the Liberty County Jail in Liberty, Texas. I also spent a week at a shelter where migrants are held in Los Fresnos, Texas, operated by International Educational Services, and a similar shelter in San Diego, California.

Corrections Corporation of America has denied allegations that the children in its custody were not adequately fed; however, the jail in Liberty, Texas, operated by Corrections Corporation of America no longer houses immigrant children. Immigrant children detained by the Border Patrol entering the country illegally are now handled by the Office of Refugee Resettlement within the U.S. Department of Health and Human Services, an agency that uses jails sparingly and favors more nurturing open shelters and foster care.

I retraced Enrique's run along Zacate Creek, past a sewage treatment plant, and up an embankment into a residential area on the outskirts of Laredo.

The description of how Border Patrol agents spot suspect vehicles comes from Alexander D. Hernández, supervisory agent for the Border Patrol at Cotulla, Texas, during a patrol along the same stretch of highway in south Texas that Enrique's smugglers used.

The depictions of how Enrique bypassed the Border Patrol checkpoint come, in part, from my observations during a visit to the checkpoint.

Descriptions of Lourdes's life in North Carolina and of her photos are from Lourdes, her boyfriend, and other immigrants who lived with them. She showed me the photos of her children. The account of Enrique's calls from Dallas to his mother comes from Enrique, his mother, and her boyfriend.

The account of the ride from Florida to North Carolina is based on my observations as I retraced the North Carolina portion of the trip. Details of Enrique's reunification and conversations come from Enrique, his sister Diana, Lourdes, and my observations as Enrique retraced his steps into the house, into the kitchen, down the hallways, and into his mother's room.

8. PERHAPS A NEW LIFE

The account of the reaction by María Isabel to Enrique's arrival in North Carolina comes from Belky, her aunt Rosa Amalia, María Isabel, and her aunt Gloria.

The account of Enrique's job, earnings, and purchases is from my observations.

For the depiction of Enrique's life in North Carolina with Lourdes between 2000 and 2005, I spoke with Enrique, a fellow painter and friend, Enrique's boss, Lourdes, her boyfriend, the boyfriend's son, the boyfriend's brother, Lourdes's daughter Diana, and her sister Mirian.

Stories about the relationship between Enrique and his mother, including the resentment of immigrant children at having been left behind, are from Enrique, Lourdes, Diana, Lourdes's boyfriend, and his cousin, as well as Maria Olmos, principal of the Newcomer Center at Belmont High School, a school for immigrants in Los Angeles; Gabriel Murillo, a former counselor at Belmont; and Aldo Pumariega, the principal of the now-closed Bellagio Road Newcomer School in Los Angeles.

María Isabel's decision to follow Enrique was related to me by María Isabel, her aunt Gloria, and her mother, Eva.

9. THE GIRL LEFT BEHIND

The accounts of life for Enrique, María Isabel, Lourdes, her sister Mirian, and others are based on my trip to Honduras and North

Carolina in 2003 and interviews with Enrique, Lourdes, and members of their families in Honduras and in the United States between 2000 and 2005.

Additional information comes from Enrique's maternal and paternal grandmothers, his sister Belky, his aunt Rosa Amalia, his uncle Carlos, and Lourdes's cousin María Edelmira.

I spent a week in 2003 observing the lives of María Isabel and her daughter, Jasmín, in Honduras. I spent time at each of the three homes where María Isabel had lived in Tegucigalpa.

To better understand Los Tubos, the neighborhood where María Isabel lived with her mother, I took a tour of the area with Reina Rodríguez and María Isabel Sosa of the local health clinic, the Centro de Salud El Bosque. Oscar Orlando Ortega Almendares of the health center provided a history of the neighborhood and of María Isabel's family. I spoke with José Luis Pineda Martínez, the director of the local school María Isabel attended, the Escuela 14 de Julio. I interviewed Cydalia de Sandoval, president of the Asociación Damas de la Caridad San Vicente de Paúl, which runs a local daycare center and orphanage, and Argentina Valeriano, owner of the neighborhood bodega, the Pulpería Norma. I accompanied María Isabel to her job at the children's clothing store.

The description of María Isabel's life in Honduras is from María Isabel; her sister Rosario; her brother Miguel; her mother, Eva; and her aunt Gloria. Suyapa Valeriano, who lives near Eva's home in Los Tubos and took phone calls from Enrique for María Isabel, also provided details.

The description of Honduras's economic and social conditions comes from Maureen Zamora, a migration expert in Honduras; Marta Obando at UNICEF's Honduras office; Norberto Girón with the International Organization for Migration; Glenda Gallardo, the principal economist, and Alex Cálix, the director of national development information, at the United Nations Development Program in Honduras; Francis Jeanett Gómez Irias, a social worker with the Instituto Hondureño de la Niñez y la Familia; Nubia Esther Gómez, a nurse with the program; and Leydi Karina López, the head of human resources of S.J. Mariol, a clothing factory in Tegucigalpa. I also consulted documents in the UNICEF library in Tegucigalpa.

10. UNEXPECTED REUNIONS

The description of María Isabel's trip to reach Enrique comes from interviews I held with her. Information about the events that occurred after she arrived in Florida was given to me by Enrique, María Isabel, and Lourdes.

I appeared on the *Don Francisco Presenta* show with Lourdes, Enrique, and Belky.

EPILOGUE

I visited with the family in Florida both in 2011 and 2012, in addition to conducting regular telephone interviews with them between 2000 and 2012. I interviewed them about their lives and experiences with crime during their stay at an apartment there. I also interviewed Enrique at the Florida detention center and reviewed arrest records.

Only Washington and New Mexico allow unlawful immigrants to obtain driver's licenses.

The statistics on Florida doubling the amount of undocumented immigrants comes from U.S. Immigration and Customs Enforcement (ICE) at the Department of Homeland Security. ICE provided the information about the amount of money the detention center where Enrique was held receives per immigrant inmate, as well as a tour of the facility.

The information about how Zeta enforcers harass and kill people in Honduras comes from interviews with people in Enrique's old neighborhood.

I conducted interviews with Belky and other family members in Honduras via telephone between 2000 and 2012.

I visited the motel, where Enrique was arrested, and the hospital where Daniel Enrique was born. On September 23, 2012, I visited Lourdes's evangelical church and went with Lourdes, Jasmín, and Daniel to visit Enrique in jail.

I interviewed both attorneys representing Enrique.

AFTERWORD

The number of undocumented children in the United States is from a December 2011 Pew Hispanic Center study by Paul Taylor, Mark Hugo Lopez, Jeffrey S. Passell, and Seth Motel entitled "Unauthorized Immigrants: Length of Residency, Patterns of Parenthood."

The statistics on the number of immigrant children or children of immigrants in the nation's schools is from a 2010 study by Karina Fortuny, Donald J. Hernandez, and Ajay Chaudry entitled "Young Children of Immigrants: The Leading Edge of America's Future."

The events in Nuevo Laredo were reported by local newspaper *El Mañana* and other news organizations.

A 2012 Amnesty International report, "Invisible Victims: Migrants on the Move in Mexico," detailed how forty Central American migrants were abducted from a train in Medias Aguas, Veracruz, by Zeta gang members. Amnesty International also reported the discovery of 193 bodies of Central American migrants who had been killed and placed in clandestine graves. The interviews with migrants who told of local Mexican officials' involvement in the crime against Central American migrants are from the Comición Nacional de Derechos Humanos report entitled

"Informe Especial sobre Sequestro de Migrantes en México 2010." Details covering abuses suffered by Central American migrants in Mexico were provided by the Human Rights Watch World Report 2012: Mexico and the Amnesty International Report.

The assertion that there are more pregnant women and young children on the trains comes from Julio César Cancino Gálvez, of Grupo Beta Sur, and Olga Sánchez Martínez, who runs a shelter for the injured in Chiapas.

The previous and current numbers of Central American migrants detained and deported by Mexico are from a July 2011 report from Mexico's Immigration Institute, the Instituto Nacional de Migración.

The U.S. Border Patrol detained 56,637 non-Mexican migrants, mostly Central American, between October 2011 and May 2012—more than double the 27,561 detained the same period a year earlier.

The information regarding a friend of Enrique's who boarded a train in Chiapas crowded with 1,500 other migrants is from a September 2012 interview I conducted with the friend.

The number of unaccompanied Central American minors traveling into the United States comes from U.S. Customs and Border Protection. The number of unaccompanied Mexican minors comes from Mexico's Ministry of Foreign Affairs.

To reach the estimate of about 100,000 children who enter the U.S. from Central America and Mexico each year illegally and without either parent, I added the following numbers: The U.S. Department of Health and Human Services, which takes custody of apprehended children, detained 14,000 non-Mexican children in fiscal 2012. Mexico's Ministry of Foreign Affairs expects the U.S. government to deport more than 16,000 unaccompanied Mexican minors. Representative Lamar Smith, chair of the House Judiciary Committee, which has custody of the immigration issue, has estimated that two to four migrants get in for every one migrant apprehended.

Kids In Need of Defense, a nonprofit organization that provides pro bono legal aid to unaccompanied migrant minors, provided information about how the U.S. government dealt with the surge in unaccompanied minors.

The information regarding anti-immigrant legislation in multiple U.S. states was provided by the National Conference of State Legislatures in an August 2012 report entitled "2012 Immigration-Related Laws and Resolutions in the States" as part of their Immigration Policy Project.

Accounts of Lourdes's and Enrique's views on life in the United States, and their views on immigration, are derived from interviews I conducted with them between 2000 and 2012.

A 2011 study by the Pew Research Center called "Wealth Gaps Rise to Record Highs Between Whites, Blacks, and Hispanics," by Paul Taylor, Rakesh Kochnar, Richard Fry, Gabriel Velasco, and Seth Motel, details the 66 percent drop in household wealth for Hispanic households.

Steven A. Camarota from the Center for Immigration Studies says in his October 2011 study "A Record-Setting Decade of Immigration: 2000–2010" that a total of 27.2 million immigrants, legal and illegal, arrived in the United States between 1990 and 2010. He ascertains that the immigration rate in the decade from 2000 to 2010 was the highest in American history.

I spent time during 1999 and 2000 at Los Angeles's Newcomer School, where I interviewed dozens of mothers and children and attended classes and student therapy and counseling sessions.

The estimate that immigrants in the United States send $40 billion to Latin America is from the Inter-American Development Bank.

The U.N. Office on Drugs and Crime in 2007 said there were an estimated 36,000 gangsters in Honduras.

A February 1, 2011, report by the Pew Hispanic Center entitled "Unauthorized Immigrant Population: National and State Trends, 2010," by Jeffrey S. Passel and D'Vera Cohn, reported that the number of illegal immigrants entering the United States has plunged by almost two-thirds in the past decade, going from an average of 850,000 entering each year between 2000 and 2005 to 300,000 entering each year between 2007 and 2009.

The percentages on the current foreign-born population in the United States come from "The Foreign-Born Population in the United States: 2010" report by the U.S. Census Bureau. The Census Bureau's 2010 American Community Survey reported that 27 percent of California residents were born in another country.

The 1997 National Research Council study cited is entitled "The New Americans: Economic, Demographic, and Fiscal Effects of Immigration." The 2003 Harvard University study about immigrant effects on wages is "The Labor Demand Curve Is Downward Sloping: Reexamining the Impact of Immigration on the Labor Market," by George J. Borjas, professor of economics and social policy at the John F. Kennedy School of Government.

I refer to stories in the *Los Angeles Times*: "For This Union, It's War," August 19, 1993, and "Natives, Newcomers at Odds in East L.A.," March 4, 1996.

The 1997 RAND study that discusses the excessive number of immigrants is "Immigration in a Changing Economy: The California Experience," by Kevin F. McCarthy and Georges Vernez.

The U.S. Customs and Border Protection reports that it has more than 21,000 offices, which is more than five times the 4,000 offices it had when the crackdown on immigration began in 1993. According to the U.S. Government Accountability Office, in a March

30, 2011, report entitled "Border Security DHS Progress and Challenges in Securing the U.S. Southwest and Northern Borders," the U.S. spent $11.9 billion on border security in fiscal 2010. The U.S. Customs and Border Protection also reports, as of February 2012, that it has completed 651 miles of wall along the Southwestern border.

Miriam Jordan reported in a May 2, 2012, *Wall Street Journal* article, "Fresh Raids Target Illegal Hiring," on the "silent raids" conducted by Immigration and Customs Enforcement on five hundred businesses "of all sizes and types." The information about the ease of illegal immigrant workers reusing social security cards and names comes from my interviews with meatpacking plant workers in Colorado and Kansas.

The Georgia Fruit and Vegetable Growers Association commissioned a University of Georgia study that found estimated crop losses of about $140 million due to Georgia's new immigration law. With the multiplier effect, it calculated about $390 million in lost economic activity for the state.

In their report "Smuggling of Migrants," the United Nations Office on Drugs and Crime estimates that 90 percent of illegal migrants are assisted by smugglers. The U.S. Border Patrol saw 368 migrant deaths in 2011.

The U.S. Border Patrol reported that apprehensions of illegal immigrants peaked in 1986 at 1.69 million but dropped to 340,252 in fiscal 2011, the lowest level since 1971.

The statistics about Mexican fertility come from Dowell Myers, a professor of Public Policy at the University of Southern California.

The information on the percentage of Honduran children who never attend school comes from the Honduras National Institute of Statistics report "Evolución de Algunos Indicadores de Educación en la Población de 3 a 17 años en Honduras, 2010."

The International Organization for Migration provided the statistics for worldwide migration. A March 2011 report titled "Unaccompanied Children in Europe: Issues of Arrival, Stay and Return" from the Parliamentary Assembly Council of Europe provided information on unaccompanied minors.

ACKNOWLEDGMENTS

Much of the original research for this book was done for the series of articles titled "Enrique's Journey" that I wrote for the *Los Angeles Times*. I am particularly indebted to my editor there at the time, Rick Meyer. Rick is the best editor a reporter could hope for. He is incredibly supportive and demands that a story meet the highest journalistic standards. His infectious enthusiasm for a good yarn makes you try to do your best work. He taught me more about how to tell a story than any other editor I've had. It is no mystery why reporters clamor to work for Rick.

I would also especially like to thank the former executive editor of the *Los Angeles Times,* John Carroll, who believed in "Enrique's Journey" from the beginning and who painstakingly and skillfully edited twelve drafts of the series of articles. John's eyes light up at the thought of rolling up his sleeves, pencil in hand, and finding ways to make each part of a story better. I am also indebted to John for giving me the time off to expand the series into the original adult edition of this book.

I am thankful to the dozens of people at the *Los Angeles Times,* too many to name, who were also instrumental in improving this story. These include people who worked on editing, copyediting, photography, research, graphics, design, Web presentation (including multimedia efforts), and the Spanish-language translation of the series for the Web.

At Random House, I want to thank David Ebershoff, editor of the adult edition of *Enrique's Journey,* for facilitating the young adult adaptation, and Beverly Horowitz, vice president and publisher of Delacorte Press, for her passion for this book.

I thank my agent, Bonnie Nadell, who gave me the initial nudge to write this book and whose support and wise counsel helped immeasurably throughout. My research assistant, Rosario Parra, helped edit and proofread this edition. I want to thank her for everything she does to keep my writing life on course.

Hundreds of people helped me in the process of researching and writing this book. Some in particular gave me an extraordinary amount of their time and effort. First and foremost are Enrique, Lourdes, and María Isabel. Enrique and Lourdes agreed to cooperate despite the obvious dangers. As illegal immigrants, they took a real risk. All they had were my assurances that I would tell their story faithfully and to the best of my abilities, and that doing so might help others understand what families like theirs go through and what the migrant journey is like. For them, this project was a leap of faith. They gave me weeks of their time over the course of five years and have given additional time and interviews in the subsequent six years, putting up with endless probing questions, with little more than the hope that I would clearly and accurately convey their experiences. I cannot thank them enough.

I want to thank their families in the United States and in Honduras, who were equally open and patient with me. In the United States, I am indebted to Lourdes's boyfriend and to Diana. The book would not have been possible without the generous help in

Honduras of Belky, Rosa Amalia, Mirian, Carlos Orlando Turcios Ramos, Tania Ninoska Turcios, Karla Roxana Turcios, María Edelmira Sánchez Mejía, Ana Lucía, María Marcos, Águeda Amalia Valladares, Gloria, and Eva. I thank Mexico's train companies—Ferrocarriles Chiapas-Mayab, Transportación Ferroviaria Mexicana, and Ferrosur—for allowing me to ride on their trains. Virginia Kice and others at what was then called the Immigration and Naturalization Service helped me gain access to jails and shelters where migrant children were held. At one of those shelters in Texas, International Educational Services, program coordinator Ruben Gallegos, Jr., helped me interview dozens of migrant children.

In Chiapas, Grupo Beta Sur, and specifically agent Julio César Cancino Gálvez, helped me safely access some of the most dangerous spots where migrants travel, including the train tops. Olga Sánchez Martínez and her family took me into their home and showed me true generosity. Others who gave much of their time in Chiapas were Olivia Ruiz, Hugo Ángeles Cruz, Jorge Reinoso, Gabriela Coutiño, and Sara Isela Hernández Herrera.

In Nuevo Laredo, I thank Padre Leonardo López Guajardo and four nuns who are instrumental to his work: Sisters Elizabeth Rangel, María del Tepeyac, Leonor Palacios, and Juanita Montecillo. I also want to thank human rights activist Raymundo Ramos Vásquez.

In Texas, Border Patrol trackers Charles Grout and Manuel Sauceda gave me invaluable insights. In Los Angeles, I owe much of my understanding of how these separations hurt families to former Newcomer School counselor Gabriel Murillo.

Finally, the person I most want to thank is my husband, Bill Regensburger, who endured my long absences as I reported this book and who has always been a loving, patient, and ardent supporter of my work.

ABOUT THE AUTHOR

SONIA NAZARIO has spent more than twenty years reporting and writing about social issues, most recently as a projects reporter for the *Los Angeles Times*. Her stories have tackled some of this country's most intractable problems: hunger, drug addiction, and immigration.

Ms. Nazario has won numerous national journalism and book awards. Her *Los Angeles Times* series "Enrique's Journey" won more than a dozen awards, among them the Pulitzer Prize for feature writing, the Grand Prize of the Robert F. Kennedy Journalism Award, and the National Association of Hispanic Journalists Guillermo Martinez-Marquez Award for Overall Excellence. She is on the board of Kids In Need of Defense, a nonprofit organization launched by the Microsoft Corporation and Angelina Jolie to provide pro bono legal counsel to unaccompanied immigrant children.

Sonia Nazario lives in Los Angeles.